A HORSE IN THE MORNING

Stories from a sometimes unusual life.

By

ROGER LEY

Copyright © 2015 Roger Ley

All rights reserved

No part of this publication may be reproduced, stored in a retrieval system, or transmitted, in any form or by any means, without the prior permission of the author, nor be otherwise circulated in any form or binding or cover other than that in which it is published and without a similar condition including this condition being imposed on the subsequent purchaser.

This book is of non-fiction based on experiences and recollections of the author. Names have been changed to protect the privacy of individuals.

Every reasonable effort has been made to trace copyright holders of material reproduced in this book, but if any have been inadvertently overlooked the author would be glad to hear from them.

Cover copyright © 2015 Roger Ley

ISN: 1515120856
ISBN-13: 978-1515120858

For my sons and my grand children.

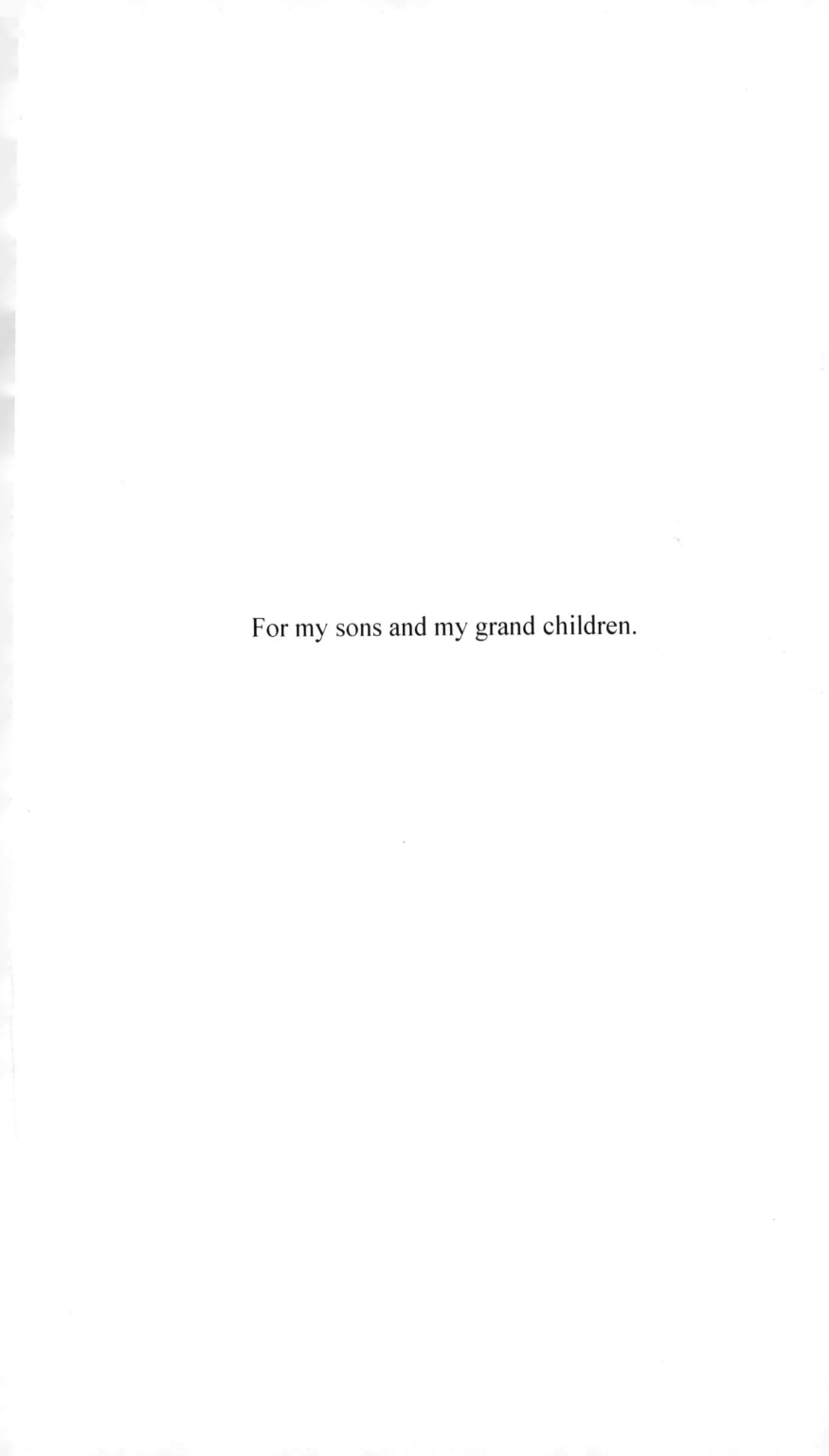

CONTENTS

PART ONE CHILDHOOD

Introduction
Chapter 1 1953 My First Memory
Chapter 2 1954 The Whistling Virgin
Chapter 3 1959 The Train Home from Dolgellau
Chapter 4 1961 I Once Met Tony Hancock
Chapter 5 1963 The Tin Man and the Thirteenth Apostle
Chapter 6 1964 The Long Drop Latrine
Chapter 7 1966 Dog Days
Chapter 8 1967 I Once Met Graham Hill
Chapter 9 1967 My First Car was a BMW
Chapter 10 1967 The Drowning Farmer
Chapter 11 1969 Pete Love and the Angel of Death

PART TWO YOUTH

Chapter 12 1969 The Stream of Fire
Chapter 13 1974 I Start Working in the Oilfields
Chapter 14 1975 Arrested at Tripoli Airport
Chapter 15 1975 Nick Poole's Nice Pink Party Frock
Chapter 16 1975 Wally the Welder's Poorly Bad Foot
Chapter 17 1975 The Wreck of the Francis Holmes
Chapter 18 1975 The Bar at Zueitina Terminal
Chapter 19 1976 Inside the Engine and the Desert Djinn
Chapter 20 1976 Working Offshore
Chapter 21 1976 Echo Fisk
Chapter 22 1977 The Desert Song
Chapter 23 1977 Aberdeen Airport
Chapter 24 1978 The Girl on the Underground Platform

PART THREE MANHOOD

Chapter 25 1980 Alternative Solutions
Chapter 26 1982 Dowsing
Chapter 27 1984 A Memorable Character
Chapter 28 1985 The Child is Father to the Man
Chapter 29 1994 Inside Blundeston Prison
Chapter 30 1997 A Crossing to Bardsey Island
Chapter 31 2006 Doing Something Slightly Dangerous

PART FOUR RETIREMENT

Chapter 32 2008 The Autocad Diaries
Chapter 33 2009 The Park Inn Hotel In Berlin
Chapter 34 2011 Filming 'A Mother's Son'
Chapter 35 2012 The Horse in the Morning
Chapter 36 2014 Electric Shadows
Chapter 37 2015 The Secret World Of Cinderella

AFTERWORD

APPENDICES
Appendix 1 Rejection for astronaut training - NASA about 1972
Appendix 2 Explosion on the Francis Holmes 1
Appendix 3 Explosion on the Francis Holmes 2
Appendix 4 Family recipe, won food competition in the Guardian
Appendix 5 Your baby has gone down the plughole
Appendix 6 List of articles previously published.

ILLUSTRATIONS

Many of the photographs in this book spent fifty years in attics where the temperature was far too hot in the summers for the good of their emulsion. They have all been scanned now but the quality of some of them is not as good as I would have liked.

Introduction My mother and father first meet
Chapter 1 The Ley family 1955
Chapter 6 The Ley family in Aden
Chapter 6 Shark notice at Tarshyne sports club
Chapter 6 Teenagers lounging at the pool at our sports club
Chapter 6 Saleh Muhammed Ali the sheik's representative
Chapter 6 The charging elephant
Chapter 6 Lions in the game park outside Nairobi
Chapter 7 The author in his Sea Scout uniform
Chapter 7 Scouts on parade at Rowallan camp
Chapter 8 Cutting from The Times about the Junior Wings scheme
Chapter 9 Isetta 300 bubble car
Chapter 10 Me the three girls and my brother Nick
Chapter 13 The author next to one of the turbo pumps at Zueitina
Chapter 15 Nick Poole and myself working on a turbo pump
Chapter 17 The wreck of the Francis Holmes
Chapter 17 Scuba diving from the Crab
Chapter 19 TA gas turbine with combustion chamber at the front
Chapter 28 Santa and the Ley boys at Selfridges
Chapter 30 A meal of beer, bread and lobster with James
Chapter 32 ND2 present me with a battle scarred AutoCAD manual
Chapter 33 The Park Inn and base jumping concession
Chapter 34 Filming in Southwold
Chapter 36 My equine visitor
Chapter 37 Llama temple roof detail
Chapter 37 A Beijing street musician
Chapter 37 Whipping a spinning top in the park in Xian
Chapter 38 Angina & Verucca in the Cinderella pantomime

Foreword

1949 I AM BORN AND HAVE A BRIEF ENCOUNTER WITH QUEEN MARY

Aged 0

Although my father spent most of the Second World War as a non commissioned officer in the RAF, he gained the King's commission in 1945. This meant that my mother was allowed to give birth to me in the Officers Hospital in Hampstead in January 1949. This was a suitable environment for me to make my entrance into the world.

Soon after my birth, Queen Mary, the Queen Mother at that time and widow of King George V, visited the hospital. Queen Mary was a Princess of Teck in Wurttemberg although she had been brought up in England.

She entered my mother's room and having peered diffidently into my crib asked my mother, 'Why is this baby wearing white mittens?'

It is interesting to reflect on this statement because Queen Mary had given birth to six children of her own.

Perhaps hers had worn swaddling clothes or perhaps she just hadn't had much to do with them.

'To stop him from scratching his face your majesty, babies aren't in control of their limbs and their nails can be sharp.'

'Oh,' said Queen Mary, 'I always wondered why my great grandson Charles wears white mittens.'

Disappointingly this was to be my closest and only connection with the British Royal Family. For that brief moment I was in synchronicity with an heir to the throne, but as time went by our paths diverged. He became hugely rich and famous, I did not. He married a woman who became a princess, I did not.

PART ONE CHILDHOOD

And the Sixties

Roger Ley

Introduction

THE BUDDING OF A NEW BRANCH.

This photograph was taken in 1941, during the Second World War, outside a church in Liverpool. It shows my mother and father, who had never previously met, shortly after he had invited her to, 'Come and have your photograph taken with me.' As can be seen, my father is a corporal in the RAF at the time, and is the best man at the wedding of one of his friends. They were both Morse code radio operators. He is holding the groom's forage cap and wearing his own as far over to the right as possible without it falling off as was de rigueur at the time.

My mother and father first meet

My father's ruse worked well, he and my mother were soon an 'item' and later they became engaged. At the time that the photograph was taken, my mother was serving an apprenticeship in the fabric department of the

Lewis department store in Liverpool. Unfortunately the week that she completed her training and picked up her first full wage, the store was bombed and she lost her job. She left the dangers of the bombings in Liverpool and joined the WRAF, where she felt relatively safe and quickly put on a healthy stone in weight after joining up. Coming from a large family she had always had enough to eat, but there was never more than a sufficiency. In the WRAF, unbelievably, she found that she could go back for a second helping at mealtimes.

My parents were married in 1942 and their union produced four sons, seven grandchildren and, so far, three great grandchildren. I know that this is not particularly unusual but it is not often that a camera captures the very moment that a branch of a family tree first begins to bud.

At the time of writing my mother is ninety-five years old and lives in her own flat. Unfortunately, my father died in 1972

Chapter 1   1953 MY FIRST MEMORY

Aged 4

The Coronation of Queen Elizabeth II.

In 1953 there were only three car owners on Whitehouse Avenue, the street where I was brought up. There were few families that owned a television, only one that my parents knew anyway. In those days a television aerial attached to the chimney of your house was an important status symbol.

I sat in a darkened room with about fifteen other people peering at the small black and white screen, mounted in its walnut veneered cabinet, and watched the coronation of Queen Elizabeth II. My parents weren't there because they had gone to London to join the celebrating crowds. I was in the care of my Aunty Peggy and was duly spoiled with milk and biscuits. Of course, I have seen the repeat so many times since, that now I am not sure where my original memory ends and my later memories overlap, but I remember being there at Aunty Peggy's and watching the crown being placed on the Queen's head. Although, at the time, I wasn't actually sure who she was, I was only four after all.

Whatever my personal views about the Royal Family and the idea of a constitutional monarchy, I will miss our Queen when she passes on. During my lifetime, politicians have come and gone, but whichever schools I have attended, jobs I have laboured at, children I have raised, the Queen has always been there in the background, rather like a distant grandparent. Her coronation is my first memory and her presence during my whole lifetime has provided a certain continuity to my life and to the life of this country.

Chapter 2   1954 THE WHISTLING VIRGIN

Aged 5

'I know how to go home on my own.'

At the age of five my parents enrolled me at St Teresa's infant school in Borehamwood; it was run by two Dominican nuns and was established in a large green wooden hut, which stood on the site now occupied by St Teresa's Catholic Church. One day, when we were studiously involved in the theory and practice of plasticine modelling, one of the little girls began to whistle.

'Girls should not whistle Pauline,' Sister Veronica said in her gentle Irish brogue.

'Why not sister?'

'Because, child, Our Lady didn't whistle.'

This was powerful stuff and I wondered if boys were allowed to whistle. I couldn't imagine Jesus whistling, particularly as I had mainly seen him nailed to a cross, so I decided not to take the risk. It might be a 'mortal sin,' this would leave a stain on my soul which would mean that, on my demise, my childish mistake would require that I be removed to hell to be subjected to eternal damnation and torment because, of course, we have an 'all forgiving and merciful God,' who loves us all, especially little children. I went home for lunch and my mother asked me about my morning. I told her that Sister Veronica had said that the Virgin Mary didn't whistle.

'How does she know? Was she there two thousand years ago or did somebody write it down?' This brought a whole new perspective of doubt to my childhood religious beliefs, which up until then had been as solid and unquestioning as my belief in Father Christmas. How does she know? I asked myself and quietly began to question the whole shaky structure.

The Ley family about 1955 - I am on the far right

Eventually, the green hut was removed to allow room for a new Catholic church. A proper new St Teresa's primary school was built nearby into which we were all recruited along with a lot of new kids. Its walls were built of yellow bricks, which were soft enough to bore a hemispherical hole into with the use of a penny or a sixpence coin when there was nothing else to do in the playground. I wonder how much of it has been bored away like this since its opening more than fifty years ago. It ought to look like a Swiss cheese by now. The building was very sixties: airy, light with parquet flooring and interesting modernistic wallpaper. The teachers were enthusiastic, almost exclusively Irish, and Catholic of course. Onto the scene came the school's first headmaster, Mr Bateman. He was a wonderful man; hurriedly gulping his tea at the back of the hall and spilling it down the front of his suit before assembly, he would sometimes burst unannounced into lessons and take over from the teacher with quizzes, jokes, or stories, always delivered at break neck speed in his Southern Irish accent.

'Well children, a baby was born in Ireland with a full head of hair and a full set of teeth. It bit the mother on the breast while she was feeding it.'

Horrified pause and transfixed stares from the audience.

'They called the priest to pray over the baby to exorcise it and, as he sprinkled the Holy Water on its head, it screamed to high heaven as the 'Divil' came out of it.'

Yes, I thought but what about its hair and teeth? Did they go back to normal?

One day, during the lunch break, I went into the old church next door to the school probably to say ten Hail Mary's in the hope of improving my chances of passing the 11 plus exam and being selected to go to grammar school. The old church would eventually be relegated for use as a church hall when the modern new church was built. It had dried out plaster with large cracks running across the high ceilings, the usual benches, altar and, of course, a large crucifix hung above the altar back lit by the east window behind it. There was a group of four small girls all about seven years old in St Teresa's school uniform grey skirt and blouse kneeling at the front of the church. Suddenly, one of a group of them screamed, 'His head moved.'

Apparently the large statue of Jesus on the cross, above the altar, had previously been looking to the right, but was now looking to the left. Neither pupils nor teachers who came to investigate the commotion could honestly remember which way the statue had been looking originally and all three of the girls swore that they had seen the statue's head turn around. So, it must have been a miracle!

Talking of miracles, I am reminded of the story of the priest who was showing a rabbi around Lourdes. While explaining the miraculous cures, he pointed to a pile of discarded crutches. 'Ah,' said the rabbi nodding his head, 'but no false legs.'

One day, Mr Bateman was showing the parents of a prospective pupil around the school when they expressed concern about what sort of accent their son would pick up at St Teresa's.

'I'll just pick a child at random,' Mr Bateman said, pointing at me, knowing full well what sort of accent I had, thanks to my father's constant corrections.

'Girilt, (my name was Gerald) say after me, "I know how to go home on my own."'

I did, and in my best 'in front of my Dad BBC English' accent.' The parents were impressed, and the boy was duly enrolled. Later, I heard 'Mr B' telling the story to teachers on a couple of occasions, and chuckling as he did so, while nodding in my direction. I felt that I had been used in some way. I still liked Mr Bateman, but he did go down a bit in the estimation of my ten-year-old self. Adults often make the mistake of thinking that things are going over children's heads when they are not.

Immediately after I left St Teresa's at the age of eleven, sadly he died of a brain tumour. The management of the school was taken over by nuns.

'Get away,' shouted the senior nun out of a window at the three of us standing quietly at the school gate, a few months later. 'We don't want you here.'

A couple of my friends and I had only wanted to visit our Alma Mater to show off our smart new Grammar school uniforms. Something encouraged, under the previous regime, as it gave the younger kids something to aspire to. Feeling like criminals, Mickey McDonough, Michael Shanahan and I slunked away.

The only unhappy incident that I remember from St Teresa's was when the pretty, new teacher, Miss Jones, came to take our class one morning. Two of the boys got on her nerves so she made them stay after the lesson. She sat them down on opposite sides of a child sized table, and told Paddy McGovern to place his hands over those of Michael Fitzgerald and to hold them down. Standing behind Paddy she proceeded to enthusiastically slap Michael's face several times while his friend prevented him from defending himself, then she reversed the situation. The psychologically nasty part of this punishment was the way that she had forced each boy to be complicit in the punishment of his friend. They both seemed unusually shaken by the experience as we stood around, drinking our morning bottles of milk. I wonder where she learned this technique.

Every Saturday my father sent me, my younger brother Nick, and my older brother Brian, to Confession. Brian had been a regular smoker since the age of seven and felt himself too far gone in sin by the time he was twelve, to ever be redeemed. We would stop a couple of hundred yards from the church in an overgrown wooded area where a stream emerged from under the road, issuing from a large concrete pipe which I would never have the nerve to explore but always wanted to. There was a British Legion building nearby but it was an area usually free from the prying eyes of adults, with plenty of dry sticks lying around for making camp fires, we played there regularly. On Saturdays, Brian would wait there, sitting in the bushes smoking while, unbeliever though he was, he oversaw us younger ones doing our Catholic duty and attending weekly Confession to have our sins absolved. What a useful instrument Confession is, because how would a priest know what was going on in his patch if the parishioners didn't go and tell him all about their sinful activities every week? On one occasion a priest was obviously disappointed with my list of negligible misdemeanours and asked my eleven-year-old self if I'd had any unclean thoughts about women. Realising what was expected of me I answered that I had. He asked me how I had thought about them.

'With nothing on,' I told him confidently and he seemed satisfied. In fact I'd had no such thoughts but I said the 'Hail Marys' anyway.

One day after I had gone to the church, confessed to Father Murray that I had said, 'Shit,' twice and forgotten to say my morning prayers three times, got my absolution, said my ten 'Hail Marys' and returned to the stream as quickly as possible to continue to build dams with my brothers, I asked Brian, 'But what will become of you if you don't go to Confession?'

'Oh,' he said airily, 'I'll probably just be a Protestant.'

Nick and I were shocked at his careless audacity. A Protestant: unbelievable. Neither Nick nor I were actually sure what a Protestant was, but we knew that they went to a different church from us and that you were either one or the other. Rather like being a Liverpool or an Everton supporter, it was all rather mysterious. We also knew that Protestants had martyred lots of Catholics in the past. It was a great surprise to me, in later life, to discover that the Catholics had also martyred Protestants; apparently it all depended on the politics at the time. At the Catholic schools that I had attended they only ever mentioned the former, never the latter. Now I realise that they were as bad as each other.

After passing my eleven-plus exam, I moved

from the lovely safe environment of St Teresa's junior school in Borehamwood, to Finchley Catholic Grammar School. An hour's travel on the 107 bus to High Barnet, and from there a trolley bus ride to the Swan and Pyramids public house in Finchley, took you back a century and a half in educational practice. What a waste of time and effort the journey was, when I could just as easily have gone to the local Grammar School, which was a mile away from our house. The problem was that my father, who was a lapsed Catholic, insisted that we followed the same questionable educational path that he had. He had been educated by priests at the Salesian College in London in the nineteen thirties, and he wanted his four sons to have a Catholic education as well.

I was rather small for my age at that time and did not like school sports at all. I remember standing in the goal mouth on the dank, wet soccer pitch, a new boy at Finchley Catholic Grammar School. Eleven years old, I was four feet six inches tall, weighed four stone six pounds and had been consigned to the position of goalie. Needless to say I had 'forgotten my kit sir,' and so was standing in the November rain, wearing my brown street shoes and grey school shorts, trying to avoid the deep puddle of water in front of me and apprehensively watching a pack of sweating oafs kicking the ball down the muddy pitch towards me, shouting unintelligible, grunting encouragement to each other. I shuddered as they came closer until finally, one oversized youth punted the sodden, heavy, mud plastered, leather ball full at me and I made, what seemed to me to be the logical decision, and stepped smartly to one side to let it pass into the net. I wasn't going home on the bus covered in mud, unfortunately my teammates didn't see it that way and I was never to play in a team game at that school again.

I was dispatched to the 'long distance runners,' code for a group of kids who had no interest in organised sports or were too idle or uncoordinated to take part even if they wanted to. It would not be 'p.c.' to mention the name that was used, by staff and pupils alike, to describe us. Every sports afternoon we would change into shorts, vests and plimsolls in our classroom and set off, a noisy pack, on our three-mile road run. After about two hundred yards, as we passed over the bridge on Laurel Way, the rest of the group turned right and ran into a grassy area on the banks of the Dollis Brook. There they would spend the afternoon, splashing in the water, building dams, climbing trees, lolling about talking and, just possibly, smoking. I, on the other hand, followed the prescribed route and did the full three-mile road run on my own. On the one occasion that I had 'bunked off' home, I had been found out and suffered the pain and indignity of being 'tolleyed' by my housemaster. The Tolley was a wide split leather strap used to beat a boy's hand. It hurt like hell.

After about an hour of slogging, the route returned me to the entrance to the grassy play area, I would call out, and the rest of the group would rejoin me for the final two hundred yard run back to school. They had run four hundred yards to my three miles. As they needed me to gauge what time they should return to the classroom for a quick change, and an early finish to the day, I was in a position to make the stipulation that it was only fair that nobody should overtake me, they usually complied. Thus, every week, I would lead the pack of deadbeats and loafers, many of whom were much taller than me and could have run much faster, back through the school gates. They would, of course, all put on a convincing act of having run the course, panting, gasping and limping, but I was always in the lead.

The games teacher came to the logical but erroneous conclusion about my long distance running talents. I was obviously the best in the year and so I was entered in an inter-school championship. I was delighted to be representing my school at anything. Like a lot of people who are not talented on the sports field and deride those who are, I was actually aching to win at a sport, but my diminutive stature had, so far, made this virtually impossible.

After the Saturday bus trip to the unfamiliar sports venue, I stood at the starting line for the North London inter-schools three-mile race, peering up at the other competitors, looming above me. Soon after we set off it dawned on me that it was going to be the usual charade. Yes, I came last, and not by a head, more like a mile. In fact, I think that everybody had gone home by the time I finished the race.

The next Sunday, at my local recreation ground, sides were being picked for a 'jumpers for goalposts,' football game. As usual I was one of the last two waiting to be chosen. 'OK' said one of the captains, 'we'll have the girl and you have him.' I don't know why I bothered.

A couple of years later, at my next school, Khormaksar Secondary in Aden I joined the Duke of Edinburgh's Award scheme and, unbelievably, they based the physical tasks, that a candidate had to achieve, on height, not age, and I found that, with a little effort, I could fulfil the requirements. My bronze 'D of E' badge was the only 'sports trophy' I gained during my time at secondary school.

A year or so later, after a growth spurt, I caught up with my year group height wise, and suddenly sports became enjoyable. I have, however, never got over my dislike of PE teachers.

I could catalogue the usual list of bullying and beatings from teachers of that era, but will restrict myself to a few examples. Fortunately I had been pre-warned by my two elder brothers, who had gone to FGS before me, so I was able to keep my head down to a large extent and avoid many of the pitfalls. In their black academic gowns, the teachers billowed about the school. They were not all bad, but there were some notably nasty types.

The chemistry master, Mr Stevenson (Stinks), would try to entice you up to his flat on the top floor of the main block for tickling sessions on his bed, if you were stupid enough to go up there. One boy who was sent up on an errand and was disinclined to the tickling, kicked Mr Stevenson in the crotch and was duly expelled for his trouble. I remember feeling a sense of injustice at this.

Mr Williams (Old Willie) taught mathematics with his favourite fourteen-year-old boy sitting on his knee. It never occurred to the rest of the class that this was unusual behaviour. We never really discussed it, either with the boy in question, or among ourselves, or with our parents. There was nothing furtive in his behaviour; other members of staff came into the classroom on occasion, and Mr Williams remained seated as he spoke to them, as did his favourite pupil.

Mr Linnane (Joe) concentrated on psychological bullying, and reduced boys to hot humiliating tears in front of their classmates, by picking on physical imperfections, such as chopped off noses or over large ears. Looking back, I cannot believe the conduct of these people; a child has no frame of reference and cannot make a judgement about dubious adult behaviour, so they tend to keep quiet in case they are at fault themselves. My parents did not hear a word about it until my brothers and I were adults.

All this child abuse was apart from the normal, officially sanctioned beatings at the hands of the housemasters, often administered with a thick leather strap called the 'Tolley' and the casual cuffing, slaps and punches from teachers during lessons. Unbelievably, Mr Stevenson (he of the tickling) was a house master and was therefore permitted to beat children with a cane while screaming angrily at them, and presumably getting all sorts of perverted pleasure from the experience. I remember listening outside the closed door of a classroom as he did this. After a minute or two of listening to the screams coming from both parties to the encounter, I remember shuddering, and continued on my way down the corridor wondering who the poor unfortunate victim was, and thankful that Stinks was not my housemaster. He presented such a pleasant demeanour to the world at large but in truth he was a sadist and a pervert. As a science teacher, he was a believer in writing notes and drawing diagrams on the board which we spent the lesson laboriously copying into our notebooks. Once a term, he took us to a laboratory to do a few demonstrations, but we never did any experiments.

One set of classrooms was a converted church. Cannon Parsons the headmaster, was an expert fund raiser and had, in fact, built the school pretty much from scratch by his collecting efforts, and so a newly built church had made this one redundant. It was in this setting that my class was learning history in the company of one of the less aggressive teachers, unfortunately his name escapes me. One of the boys was looking for something in his pencil case, it was Fox, who regularly suffered humiliation from Joe Linnane for the unforgivable sin of having a 'chopped off' nose. The history teacher decided that Fox was not paying enough attention and hit him on the back of his head hard and unexpectedly as he walked up behind him. Fox hit his face on the desk top and damaged his nose before he had time brace himself. I remember the shocking sight as he lifted his head up with his face a mess of blood, snot and tears.

'Go and clean yourself up in the bogs,' said the teacher with a sigh, not at all worried that there would be any repercussions. He continued to dictate from the book he was holding, while we, petrified and very quietly, wrote his lesson down word for word.

For me the most notable teacher at FGS was Father Richard (Dick) Dent, who literally starved his way into Heaven by living on garlic. He looked like a skeleton; his breath smelt, there were unpleasant growths on his over-large head, and his hair was falling out in clumps. One year, when an English teacher wrote a school play set in ancient Rome, one of the characters walked past a group of Christians who are waiting to be thrown to the lions, and was heard to complain of the 'terrible smell of garlic.' The whole audience (parents and pupils) understood the reference and laughed.

Eventually, so we were told, Father Dent collapsed over an electric fire one weekend, while kneeling in prayer in his small room, and died in hospital from burns allied with his general weakness. So he got his wish in the end.

Thankfully, I only had to attend this Dickensian educational nightmare for three years because the civil service posted my father to Aden, and the family followed him out there and stayed for two years. My father enrolled two of my brothers and me at the British Forces Comprehensive School at Khormaksar, which was staffed by young, keen, energetic, and properly qualified teachers. Nobody was beaten or abused; it was just a normal school.

One of my favourite childhood activities was the manufacture of explosives. This may seem a little hard to believe, but in those days, an eleven-year-old child could walk into Boots the chemist with a vague note, supposedly written by a parent, and buy sulphur and saltpetre with their pocket money. Charcoal was easily made with a small fire at the bottom of our garden and 'Bob's your uncle,' you have as much gun powder as you need to blow up bits of gas pipe, or even to repack dummy mortar bombs found on the field at the back of the film studios nearby.

Much easier and cheaper than this was to buy weed killer (sodium chlorate) from any hardware shop, and sugar at the grocers. The effects were quite similar, and you did not have to convince a pharmacist that your mum needed saltpetre to dry cure bacon, and that your dad needed the sulphur as a homeopathic remedy for the dog's digestion. The number of kids who lost hands, fingers, and worse in those days, has thankfully led to much closer control of the active substances, but in my time we made some notable explosions and got away uninjured. Perhaps I do believe in guardian angels after all.

Chapter 3   1959 THE TRAIN HOME FROM DOLGELLAU

Aged 10

'Have you had sufficient?'

As a child in the 1950s and 60s there were two choices for our family summer holiday. We either stayed at my grandparent's home in Liverpool, or we stayed with my aunt, uncle, and four cousins on their hill farm in North Wales.

Liverpool was rather a scary place for me. I was brought up in Borehamwood, and I knew how to avoid confrontations with some fairly tough kids. Survival in Liverpool, however, was more demanding. My grandparents lived in quite a pleasant terraced house and it contained treasures including, inexplicably, American comics. My grandmother, Mary Hannaway, owned a sweet shop on the docks; she sold tobacco, snuff and probably comics. My grandfather, Tommy Hannaway, was a worker on the railways. My grandmother could not stand railwaymen in general and said that they were all lazy. She kept a wooden club with nails sticking out of it next to her bed because each night she had to bring the cigarettes and other valuable stock home and hide them under her bed in case of a break in at the shop.

My grandfather worked in the shop when he was not on duty. One day a group of dockers walked past and casually ran their hands over the tops of the newspaper stands outside the shop and knocked them all over, laughing as they walked away. That evening, my grandfather tapped nails into the tops of the stands so that the points were sticking out just above the surface. The next day somebody tried to repeat the trick, but not after that. One of my abiding memories of Liverpool was that wherever there was a back wall, there was broken glass cemented on the top.

My grandfather was a quiet man but not much got past him. One day, an older boy sent his younger sister in to innocently ask for, 'A hapeth of elbow grease please Mr 'annaway.' My grandfather took the money and, having disappeared into the backyard for a moment, sent her away with a small quantity of well wrapped dog muck to give to her brother. He never played the joke again.

The favourite story about my grandmother tells of how, years before when she was a middle-aged mother of seven, she had gone to the front door one morning to collect the milk from the step. Standing on the pavement outside and eyeing the milk was the local priest.

'What a lot of milk you have there,' said the priest probably thinking that she could buy less and make a donation to the church.

'I have a lot of children Father,' said my grandmother.

'We haven't seen much of you at mass on Sundays, Mrs Hannaway.'

'I'm working out my salvation in the kitchen,' she replied and closed the door.

My mother tells of Granddad serving a not very bright young woman who had come into the shop for the first time in a little while.

'Oh Mr 'annaway, I'm married now an' everything.'

'And everything,' said my grandfather nodding as he weighed out the snuff, much to the amusement of my teenage mother, who was busy shelf stacking in the background.

As a ten-year-old, I found Liverpool to be a very different kettle of fish from where I came from. Without my support group and in unfamiliar territory, it was difficult for me to know who, on the street, was friend, and who was foe. Particularly when I found that it was very difficult to understand the local accent. As a child, I had two accents. I spoke 'BBC English' at home and, in self defence, a sort of North London 'Estuary' outside. When my brother Nick and I played in the street with local kids in Liverpool, we could no more understand some of their words than we could Welsh.

There were two parks nearby, Sefton Park and Greenbank Park. I think that it was at the former that you could hire both motorboats and rowing boats, and that was excellent fun. But it was still nerve racking to walk the mean streets of this foreign city, never knowing who was around the next corner, how many of them there were, how big they would be, or what they were talking about.

Now Wales was the other end of the holiday spectrum. I got on with my cousins; they lived on a farm with ponies to ride, and there were no other kids to worry about. There were trees to climb, streams to dam, fish to catch and cook over a camp fire. There was even a Neolithic copper mine to explore. I was thoroughly wet through all the time, of course, either because of the rain or from wading out of Wellington boot depth in pools and streams, but this was a minor concern for a ten-year-old. After tea, we would all go up the hill, sit around a campfire in one of the top fields as the evening began to darken and, as the oldest child present and family story teller, it would fall to me to provide the entertainment in the form of ghost stories designed to scare the delighted smaller cousins.

On one occasion, I remember that I came up

with a graphic account of headless men coming down from the hills and riding cattle round and round the fields until they fell dead, to the consternation of the farmers. As the tale went on the youngest of my cousins took his leave, followed by his older brother and then, progressively, his two older sisters. They all returned to the protection of the house, with its lights and adults. My younger brother Nick left and I was alone in the darkness and soon found myself running after him calling, 'Wait for me,' in a rather high and panic stricken voice.

The family sometimes took the bus to the seaside at Barmouth, and it was strange for me, as a child of the busy London suburbs, to observe the driver waiting for regular passengers who were late arriving at the bus stop.

'Mrs Jones always goes to town on Wednesday; she'll be along in a minute,' the driver would say as we waited at the stop, and lo and behold she was. Buses back home were not run on such a personal basis.

My uncle Evan was a Welsh Doctor; in fact, he was the local Medical Officer of Health, and, unlike most people, could afford a car. My aunt had been a professional actress, and the two of them had quite a 'lively' relationship, which added to the fun for us kids. My uncle had a sandy coloured moustache, often dyed purple from eating the blackberry crumbles that my aunt made. My cousins and I had to pick the blackberries. If we didn't vacate the premises immediately after lunch, my aunt could always find a job for a kid hanging around indoors.

'Just go and pick some blackberries, Gerald,' Aunty Sheila would say as she thrust a bowl into my hands. It seemed to take hours to pick a whole bowlful, and it was so boring that we didn't hang around after meals, we made ourselves scarce. At the end of the meal she would always ask, 'Have you had sufficient?'

I would always answer that I had, although it was some years before I understood what the word 'sufficient' meant in that context. Why did she not say 'enough,' I wondered?'

Even when it was raining, we could all retire to the barn near the house and play in the straw. There were ropes and ceiling beams, and I remember that we liked to play at being a circus with Nick and myself as the heroic acrobats swinging on the ropes to entertain our slightly more demure girl cousins. We loved showing off to them, and they enjoyed our company.

At the end of one summer holiday, my uncle was driving my parents, my younger brother, two cousins, and myself to the railway station at Dolgellau to catch the train home, and as usual we were a bit 'behind'. As we approached the station we could see the train just slowly pulling out. A proper train mind, a steam train, I can smell it now and see the great chuffs of steam billowing up into the roof of the station as the train had just began to move and pull itself slowly away from the platform.

As we pulled into the station car park my father, who had been brought up in London and knew a thing or two, said to me, 'Run onto the platform, go up to any man that you see in a uniform and ask him to stop the train for Dr Richards.' My father knew that Uncle Evan was a well respected, even an important local figure.

I ran onto the platform feeling that I would never get there in time and that I was going to fail the task and disappoint my father, but I found a porter and asked if he could, 'Stop the train for Dr Richards.' Unbelievably, he raised his arms and began to gesticulate, while shouting something loudly in Welsh down the platform towards the head of the train. The train slowed down, stopped and slowly reversed back into the station in a hissing cloud of steam and skidding wheels. We all got on board, and with much enthusiastic waving, began our journey home to Borehamwood as the train left Dolgellau railway station.

It was only some years later that I realised that Uncle Evan would have preferred us to catch the next train rather than presume on the good will of the porter. It was my father who had pulled rank on his behalf.

The mild mannered Uncle Evan could blow a gasket when things went wrong sometimes. On one occasion, one of us shut the car door with the keys still in the ignition. In those days, it was fairly easy to lock yourself out of a car. There was a certain amount of shouting, striding about and arm waving. I quietly went and found a knife, slid it between the rubber seal and the frame of one of the side lights, and lifted the catch to open it. With my thin little arm I was able to reach in and retrieve the keys. Proudly, I gave them to my uncle, and he thanked me, but I realised that he was rather deflated by my action. I should have let him do it rather than have a kid solve the problem for him. Nobody likes a smart ass.

He was a colourful character, my uncle Evan, a Welsh speaker, and although he was 'educated' he was, at heart, a son of the soil, and of Welsh soil to boot. He was as happy in the company of a couple of shepherds in the Cross Foxes inn as at an official dinner with a visiting dignitary at County Hall. Now that, sadly, all of my uncles have passed on, he is the one that I miss most. They would stop the train from Dolgellau for my uncle Evan.

Some years later, probably in 1980, my lovely Welsh cousin Eleanor, his daughter, died in a surprisingly minor car accident, when she suffered a fatal whiplash injury to the neck. In those days, car seats had no head support and ended at shoulder height. They seemed to be especially designed to magnify such injuries, particularly as the wearing of seat belts did not to become compulsory for another three years.

As the cortege left the Catholic Church in Dolgellau after Eleanor's funeral service, the whole town stopped as the hearse drove slowly by. Shopkeepers and customers came out of the shops and stood quietly on the pavement; men took off their hats; everybody seemed to know the family or at least of them. It was quite an eye opener for me. Nobody took a lot of notice when a funeral went by back home in Borehamwood.

Chapter 4   1961 I ONCE MET TONY HANCOCK

Aged 12

'Well he would say that, wouldn't he?'

If London Transport had extended the Northern Line of the London Underground beyond its terminus at High Barnet, the next stop would probably have been Boreham Wood or Borehamwood, as it is now called. Our family lived in an end terrace house, close to the Associated British Picture Corporation studios, usually referred to as 'Elstree Film Studios' in film credits, or just 'Elstree' if you are in 'The Business.' The studios are actually squarely in the middle of Borehamwood. Elstree, on the other hand, is rather more exclusive and five miles away. The studios are in Borehamwood though, not Elstree.

'We'd all like to have an Elstree address, Darling!'

As children, all three of my brothers and myself, had acting or stand-in work in films at 'The Studios' as the locals impartially call them. At the age of four, in 1956, my younger brother Nick, had quite a decent-sized part in a film called 'No Time for Tears' working with, among others, Silvia Syms, Anthony Quayle, Anna Neagle and Flora Robson. He played the part of Timmy, a little blind boy who had diabetes; he even had lines to say.

In later years, if ever we were having trouble with other kids being 'pushy' in the recreation grounds, I had only to say, 'He was in a film you know,' for them to stop what they were doing and want to know more. All the kids in Borehamwood were very aware of 'The Studios.'

Years later, a female colleague told me that 'No Time for Tears' was her favourite 'tear jerker'. I was quite touched that anybody still remembered it. I seem to remember that my brother Nick was paid fifty guineas for his efforts, a useful amount in those days.

The reason that we got these roles was that one of our neighbours, Mr Osborne, was a lighting technician, or an electrician, at the Studios. He had suggested my brother Nick for the part of Timmy when it became apparent that the producers could not find a suitable 'child actor' as younger relatives of established actors are known. Not that I am saying that acting is rife with nepotism. You may think that. I couldn't possibly comment.

In the summer of 1961, I was twelve and was offered three days stand-in work on a film called 'The Punch and Judy Man.' I was to be paid three guineas a day, three pounds and fifteen pence in decimal currency. They wanted my brother Nick, originally, but he was away on holiday. The film was directed by, and starred Tony Hancock, the famous comedian of stage, screen, radio and now, hopefully, film. My job was to sit under the lights while the cameramen worked out the various focus pulls, and the assistant director worked out other technical details. This could take some time, and it was considered to be too hot and tiring for the child actor, Nicholas Webb, who I was standing-in for. He was the nephew of Sylvia Syms, who played Hancock's wife in the film.

The scene that we were filming was set in an ice cream parlour, a reproduction of which had been built in the studio complete in all details including a drinks machine, refrigerators, stand-ins as customers and crucially, an ice cream machine. All that the adults around me required was that I stayed quiet and sat still, and to reinforce this behaviour they gave me ice cream, lots of ice cream. Being a reasonably intelligent child I made the connection between the ice cream and good behaviour quite quickly. So not only was I getting paid handsomely to sit and do nothing, I also had access to unlimited amounts of ice cream all day, and had the youthful metabolism to digest it without putting on significant weight. As I write this, more than fifty years later, I realise that not only was this my first job, but it was also the best job that I was ever to have during my entire working life. What a shame that it only lasted for three days.

During one of the breaks in filming, Nicholas and I were exploring the studio and had found a film set, which was supposed to be the interior of a beach hut. As we loitered beside it, the actor John Le Mesurier walked past and with his slightly faraway manner nodded and smiled vaguely to acknowledge us. Being a child I was impressed and not really used to such good manners from the generality of adults. I gained the impression, however, that Le Mesurier was so polite that he would probably have acknowledged a cat in much the same way. This was before he became famous for his role as Sergeant Wilson in the 'Dad's Army' TV series.

Work on the scene continued slowly as Mr Hancock was frequently absent, having retired to his dressing room for 'mysterious purposes,' which nobody seemed willing to talk about although they all seemed to be 'in the know.' I quietly observed this; grownups had never been so interesting. There was stifled impatience and a certain amount of hand wringing from the assistant director. The sound man, cameramen and lighting crew, who did not have to pay for the expensive studio time and were handsomely remunerated at agreed union rates irrespective of progress on the film, showed a total lack of concern. I was surprised when, after a take, the sound man actually used the 'f' word because the noise of the rotating paddles in the drinks machine had spoiled his sound track. This was the first time that I realised that adults knew about swear words. Up until then, I had thought that they were a secret confined to and passed on only by children. After all, we never used them in front of adults and, up until then, I had never heard an adult use one in front of me. Obviously my logic was flawed but then, this was my initiation into the adult world of work.

Towards the end of the scene, the child actor, Nicholas Webb, finishes eating a large sundae called a 'Piltdown Glory' and is left with a cherry in the bottom of his glass. He deftly tosses this up in the air, catches it in his mouth and eats it, with some satisfaction. The script required that Hancock copied the child's behaviour as he ate his sundae; his character was supposed to be unfamiliar with the etiquette of this activity, having never been in an ice cream parlour before. Hancock tossed a cherry up in the air out of his sundae glass several times for the camera but could never catch it in his mouth. In the end, he did catch a cherry in his mouth but fell off his bar stool in the process and spoiled the shot. There was another utterance of the 'f' word. In the end, he and the assistant director agreed to 'dub it' and so he did all the necessary actions, but with no cherry. If you watch the scene on the internet, you now know that the look of supreme satisfaction on Hancock's face after he appears to catch the cherry was pure deception.

As to my claim to fame, it is that I did act with Tony Hancock. I sat next to him to provide the background noise of a child eating a sundae, while a tight close-up was taken of him eating his confection and pulling amusing faces to camera. So, although I do not appear in the film, I am heard, and that was as close as I ever got to my 'five seconds of glory,' Piltdown or otherwise. A lasting memory that I have is of the crew applauding spontaneously whenever they judged that a shot was successful, even before the director declared it to be a 'take.'

The scene in the ice cream parlour lasts eight minutes, and took three days to make. Regretfully, after this, I was paid off and very politely escorted off the premises never to be called back to 'The Studios' - such is life.

The Wikipedia article on The Punch and Judy Man states that Mr Hancock had to wash his mouth out with Vodka between takes because he disliked the taste of ice cream.

This, of course, would explain his frequent absences from the set.

Chapter 5 1963 THE TIN MAN AND THE THIRTEENTH APOSTLE

Aged 14

The sheik was shocked that my father didn't have a hand gun.

In 1963, my civil servant father William Ley, was posted to Aden, which was still a British colony. Here he took up a job as Civilian Labour Officer at one of the big RAF bases. He had been in the RAF for a number of years before he joined the Ministry of Defence, so he knew his way around the protocols required when working with the forces. The rest of the family followed a little later at the end of the school year, except for my eldest brother Mike, who had joined the RAF.

Aden was an education for me. The poverty, the heat, the beggars and the children maimed, supposedly under Sharia law, for stealing, over the border, in the Yemen. So we were told. I never found out the truth or otherwise of this. We were also told that parents in certain tribes would dislocate their babies' hips so that they would not be able to walk properly, this would make them appear to be more pathetic, and thus more successful as beggars when they were older. Again, I never found out whether or not this was true. It may have been propaganda.

The Ley family in Aden

Aden was extremely hot and smelly, goats walked the streets eating cardboard thrown out by the shopkeepers, and if you were alone, local men would constantly offer you money for sex, presumably because the local women were locked away most of the time. It was a degenerate kind of place, more like a poverty stricken part of India than an Arab town. In fact, the British Indian Army had occupied the place for so long that the local dialect included Indian words such as 'sahib' and 'memsahib.' Men dressed in a skirt called a longyi, which is popular on the Indian subcontinent.

My brothers and I enrolled at Khormaksar Secondary School, which was a British forces comprehensive, and this was where I started and eventually completed my GCE O level course. It was a good school and, after the required fight with one of the rougher kids in my class to establish my place in the pecking order, things settled down. I was much more contented than I had been in the UK. We went to school in the morning, and then spent the afternoon at the sports club where we sunbathed on the beach, swam, and surfed or fished depending on the season. This period exactly coincided with my awakening to and sudden interest in girls. I was fourteen and what a lucky chance that I had been removed from the terrible all male Catholic grammar school and was now living in a warm environment with lots of bikini clad girls to talk to at the sports club, and fully clad ones in class. I do not remember actually having a girlfriend, although I think I made a few unsuccessful attempts. I was a bit of a photography nerd at the time, and anyway, girls of my age tended to have boyfriends who were a couple of years older than them.

Notice at the sports club beach: Sharks are silly creatures; they eat anything, boys, girls, mothers and fathers. They love visitors; Aden abounds in hungry sharks looking for a bite to eat, even if it's only a foot or leg.

The locals wanted the British to leave Aden so that they could be independent, and there was a lot of strife in the form of dissidents throwing grenades onto buses, and bombs with timers being planted in the hope of blowing up strategic buildings. Fortunately, the dissidents often stuck the time pencils into the plastic explosive the wrong way around and there were consequently quite a lot of 'might have been' bombs found. As kids, we had to check under the seats of the buses that came to take us home at the end of the school day, looking for nail bombs. These consisted of a chunk of plastic explosive, a time pencil (stolen from the British munitions stores) and a handful of six inch nails quickly gaffer taped to the underside of the bus seat. Not a complicated construction. I never found one but people I knew, both adults and children, were blown up and had the scars to prove it if they got away with it. Some did not.

Teenagers lounging by the pool at our sports club

There were several notable characters that lived in different parts of Aden colony. The 'Tin Man' lived in the town of Malla and, true to his nickname, he wore a complete suit of armour, made from large tin cans and held together with leather thongs. He left his face uncovered as he traipsed around the town carrying a stick or spear, but he wore a tin hat and a desperate expression. He lived in a hut made from forty gallon oil drums and plywood. I expect that he was suffering from some form of mental disorder. Eventually he disappeared, and I heard later that he had confronted a British Army sergeant one night with his spear and the sergeant shot him dead, with his service revolver. I am not sure whether or not this is true, but that was the gossip amongst the forces kids, and the 'Tin Man' was certainly seen no more.

The other noteworthy character was the 'Thirteenth Apostle'. I only caught sight of him once, in the street, in the port of Steamer Point. He was naked except for sandals and a loin cloth. His black hair was long, nearly down to his waist and matted with goat dung. I guess that he was in his thirties and he was whipcord thin. He walked up to a local person and asked him for money with the air of somebody who expected a contribution, rather like a Buddhist monk with his rice bowl. People would give him money quite easily; there was none of the usually shouting and whining 'baksheesh,' that accompanied begging by the locals from the British and the tourists fresh off the ships in the harbour. The giving of alms is one of the five pillars of Islam and so the 'Apostle' ignored the British and the tourists who were unlikely to be Muslims. He lived in the desert most of the time and was some sort of self styled religious visionary. I expect that he too was suffering some sort of mental disorder.

There was a war being fought 'up country' in a place called the Radfan, and even some of my scout leaders, who were all forces personnel, spent time fighting there. My father's office was blown to smithereens one day, I heard the explosion from some distance away, and it sounded like a door slamming close by. Fortunately, the dissidents were gentlemanly enough to blow up the office when he and his staff were not in it. Apparently, he was reasonably popular with the sweepers, clerks, and others that he was responsible for hiring and firing. He also took lessons in Arabic so as not to be completely at the mercy of his chief clerk, Mr Bazara, who did all the translation when people came to see my father, usually asking for a job or time off for family matters. As he had bright red hair, my father was considered to be blessed because there is a tradition that the prophet had red hair, and in Aden, when a man had made the Hajj to Mecca he would dye his hair red to signify this. Years later, when I worked in Libya, the men who had made the Hajj wore a red prayer hat and were addressed as 'Hajj'.

On a trip that he took up country, my father met the sheik of the tribe from which he recruited most of the civilian labour force. The sheik was shocked when he learned that my father did not have a hand gun, so he gave him a Beretta automatic pistol and a dozen rounds of ammunition which he brought home to our flat. I was very impressed because the first James Bond film, 'Dr No', had just been shown at the sports club, and James Bond carried a Beretta and now so too did my Dad. Well, he didn't carry it but at least he had one. Not only that but James Bond had a Rolex watch, and as Aden was a tax free port, we were all able to buy ourselves Rolex watches and camera equipment that we could never have afforded back in the UK at that time.

My father fell ill with flu, and when the sheik heard about this he must have enquired as to the correct etiquette when British people are ill. I suppose that somebody told him that it was usual to bring grapes when visiting the infirm. That evening, the sheik's right-hand man, Saleh arrived at the door of our flat with a box of grapes in his arms, so big that he could hardly carry it. The sheik had had them flown down from up-country especially. There were so many that we couldn't eat them all before they spoiled so we had to give a lot of them away.

Saleh Muhammad Ali the sheik's representative

From Aden, we were able to holiday in Kenya and go on safari. We took photos of all manner of animals and even camped in the foothills of Kilimanjaro. In the countryside, the women still walked around bare-breasted, and many of the children and the men, wore native dress. It was a world away from the way people there now live, only two generations later.

On one occasion, we were in the Tsavo game park being driven around in a Volkswagen bus, when we came upon a lone elephant. Our driver/guide told us to keep very quiet, as it was probably a grumpy old male with worn and painful teeth, who would be very bad tempered and had probably been excluded from the herd by the matriarch. (At the age of sixty-six I have some sympathy with him now.) We sat quietly; the old bull suddenly noticed us and charged down the road towards us, trumpeting impressively, huge ears flapping wildly. I was petrified. My father stood up, put his head and shoulders out of the roof and took a photograph, which is here reproduced; I admired his coolness under pressure. Our driver threw the van into reverse and drove rapidly away on the unmetalled road until we were out of range of our **short-sighted** assailant. We stopped and waited quietly until it lost interest and wandered off, but what a tale to tell when we got back to the UK. You must remember that this was before the invention of colour TV. Back in the UK, there were only a couple of TV channels to choose from and the only time that you would see any of these animals was in a zoo or a picture in a book. It was before the general population went on package holidays abroad.

My father's picture of the charging elephant

Later, when we visited the game park outside Nairobi, my father managed to pat a lion on the back through the open window of our van, as we slowly drove past. He was extremely pleased with himself for having done this, while I thought that, on that occasion, he had been foolhardy.

Lions in the game park outside Nairobi

Eventually, our posting ended and we came home to the UK. There was a choice between flying and sailing, so we sailed home on the SS Uganda. Even this journey was an eye opener: the food was wonderful; my mother collected the menus and would show them to people for years after we came home. When we stopped in Mediterranean ports, I noticed that all the married women seemed to be dressed in black, and the girls were chaperoned as they walked around the town. Years later, when I returned to Spain on holiday, I was surprised that all this had been swept aside by the march of progress. The girls wore modern clothes, they weren't chaperoned, and frequently walked around with a boy friend. Spain had become much more relaxed and like the rest of Europe, but it had not been like that in the nineteen sixties.

At the end of our journey, we arrived in the port of London. The whole of the ship's company had to stay on board and wait to go through customs and immigration. Even the first class passengers could not disembark, although presumably they would be allowed off first the next day. What a surprise for everybody, leaning over the rails, to see the Ley family, with all their luggage walking down the gang plank to be met by one of my uncles, who was a sergeant in the Flying Squad (the Sweeney.) Apparently, Uncle Frank knew the chief customs officer and, while engaging him in conversation, was surreptitiously waving us through the customs area at the exit of which my eldest brother was waiting with his car to pick us up and take us home to Borehamwood.

Had we gone through customs in the normal manner they would have found that every member of the family owned a Rolex watch; my father and I owned single lens reflex cameras; and my mother wore rather a lot of gold jewellery. Believe it or not, my father consigned his Beretta automatic pistol to the care of my thirteen-year-old younger brother, feeling that he would be the one least likely to be searched. There were no metal detectors or the like at airports in those days. Nick managed to drop the gun as we reached the car and, fortunately, as the safety catch was on, it didn't go off and shoot anybody. Dad picked it up and quickly put it in his pocket. He kept it in the top drawer of the dressing table in his bedroom for the next couple of years, which was rather good, as I could, on occasion, impress my friends with it. Teenagers, guns, what could possibly go wrong?

Eventually my father handed the gun in and it was officially destroyed; it was a different world in those days.

What a dump the UK seemed after all this adventure. The rain, all day school, homework all evening, cycling to school in the cold, our small over-crowded house on Whitehouse Avenue; I hated them all.

At least I finally found out what a Dalek was. When kids came out to Aden in the holidays and told me about 'Dr Who and the Daleks' I really could not make head or tail of it; you had to see it to understand it. I soon caught up with current British culture, and what a time it was: the Beatles, the Rolling Stones, free love (if only.)

Fortunately, my father did not make me go back to Finchley Catholic Grammar School. I enrolled at the local grammar school but flunked my A levels, probably through sheer depression, and ended up a year later at Barnet College of Further Education doing an engineering qualification, a National Diploma. I learned a lot of really useful stuff at BCFE. In later life, I would spend years teaching the same course, and always felt very committed to it and, indeed, to further education in general.

Chapter 6   1964 THE LONG DROP LATRINE

Aged 15

'Take me home, oh Muddah, Fadduh, take me home'

In the mid sixties I was a fifteen-year-old Sea Scout camping at the Rowallan Park campsite in the Ngong hills of Kenya. It was quite a lush forested area not unlike England. The troop had travelled by RAF Argosy transport plane from Aden, where our families were stationed. The Group Scout Master who was an RAF corporal had inveigled a free flight through his contacts in Air Movements.

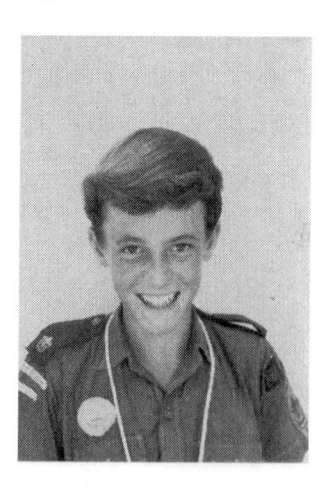

The author in his Sea Scouts uniform

The toilet arrangements at the campsite were a scattered series of small huts, each containing a large wooden box with an oval aperture cut into the top with a toilet set fixed above it. A hole had been dug below, and childish curiosity caused me to wonder how deep it was, so on the second day I took a box of matches with me and dropped a flaming bundle of toilet paper into the void; peering at it through the oval frame of the toilet seat as, with slow rotations, it fell to the bottom of the pit, about thirty feet below. At the age of fifteen, I knew nothing of the dangers of methane gas explosions. I am happy to say that nothing untoward happened, although the unpleasantness of the possibilities does not bear thinking about. In fact, the flame extinguished soon after it reached the bottom of the hole and I felt that my experiment had been a success.

It was only a couple of years later, after further study of the science of chemistry, that I realised that it had been one of the most stupid things that I had done up to that point in my young life. Although my youthful activities with weed killer and sugar pipe bombs must have run a close second. Much worse was to follow in later years.

On parade at Rowallan Camp, I am closest to the camera, the store tent is on the left

At the same camp, the troop of about twenty boys and **Scoutmasters** awoke one morning to find that a wild animal of some sort had broken into our store tent, and stolen all our sausages and some of the other meat. Later the same day, one of the younger scouts found a fully-grown baboon lying dead at the edge of the camp with its head broken open. The site superintendent examined it and explained that it was almost certainly the grisly work of a leopard. Apparently, brains make a nutritious meal for a carnivore with little chewing required and they are relatively easy to get to if the carnivore in question has a large enough gape.

That night, as I went to sleep in the marquee next to the store tent, I remember wondering about the difference in size between the head of an adult baboon and that of a medium sized boy. Not much, I thought.

'Dearest mother, darling father, here I am at Camp Granada,' went Alan Sherman's song of the time. 'Take me home, oh Muddah, Fadduh, take me home,' it continued.

Chapter 7   1966 DOG DAYS.

Aged 17

'That bloody dog!'

During the 1960's and 70's my Uncle Tony and Aunt Pat Jackson ran a pub called 'The White Hart' in Bushey, near Watford, now sadly renamed and converted to a restaurant. As children my brother Nick and I often went with my mother and father on the 107 bus from Borehamwood to Bushey on a Saturday night, so that my parents could have an evening out. My brother and I would play upstairs with my two cousins, sleep overnight and catch the bus home after breakfast the next morning. Our parents would have left the night before on the last bus.

At some point in the 1960's, a new member joined the Jackson family at the White Hart, a black Labrador dog called Sam; I can only remember him fully grown.

Sam was an intelligent fellow and soon integrated himself into the life of the White Hart. In the mornings, he would join the group of pensioners from the old people's home up the road that came down to the pub for a drink and a gossip. They would all sit around a circular table in the public bar and drink and chat, with Sam sitting on his haunches on one of the chairs looking for all the world as if he was joining in the conversation.

In reality, he was only interested in the bacon rind and other treats that came his way, but it was a comical sight much enjoyed by the other customers up at the bar. The pensioners never seemed to feel that there was anything odd about their canine recruit.

You got the impression that if they had played

cards, Sam would have a hand. My aunt and uncle had little time to take Sam for walks, so whenever one of the senior citizens decided to return to the old people's home, he would accompany them and then retrace his steps and rejoin the group back at the pub. He was a typical pub dog, friendly but not over friendly, moving from group to group when the pub was full in the evenings, and never staying long, but mingling as he felt was his duty.

Sam put on weight as he got older, and the vet advised my Aunt to cut his rations, which she duly did but with little effect. This was during the time that owners would often let dogs roam at large all day with little idea of what they were getting up to. She spoke to various customers who lived locally, and slowly a picture began to emerge of Sam's movements.

Over the years, Sam had developed a routine which involved him making a daily round of visits usually to places where he would be given 'snacks' of one sort or another. The first port of call was always the butchers next door, where he might be given a morsel or even a bone which he could take back to the pub garden for a good gnawing. An excellent way for a dog to fill the odd hour in the morning. Next was the fish and chip shop, where a few chips or some batter scratching would be on offer. I make no judgements on the suitability of Sam's diet, I merely report it.

After this, the local cafe was always good for the odd biscuit, the antique dealer was a soft touch and so it went on. He visited and was welcomed into various small businesses and private houses around the village, and hospitality was always accepted by Sam with dignified appreciation. He never overstayed his welcome; an unkind observer might suspect that this was because he was thinking of the next destination on his 'snack round' as it came to be called.

Sam integrated himself fully into the world of mankind, he gave every appearance of considering himself to be a paid up member of that particular club. One day, while my aunt was out shopping, she caught sight of him from some distance away, sitting patiently at the zebra crossing, which was a few hundred yard up the road from the White Hart.

After a few moments, the cars first on one side of the road and then on the other stopped for the canine pedestrian; passing shoppers smiled to see the dog using the crossing correctly and the drivers too were charmed and amused. Sam hoisted himself up onto his four paws and padded most of the way across the road, stopped, paused, thought better of it, turned around and much to the amusement of the onlookers and the chagrin of the drivers who had stopped in good faith, he retraced his steps back to the pavement on the original side of the street. He set off home at a reasonably brisk clip, giving the impression, if it were possible for a dog, of whistling unconcernedly as he went. He had had enough fun for one day. The car drivers, on the other hand, continued their journeys knowing that they had been outsmarted by a mutt. How infuriating for them.

'That bloody dog,' said my Auntie Pat, who was not the most patient of women, as she smoked a cigarette and told me the story, nodding towards its guilty subject, who lay quietly in his basket in the corner of the kitchen where we were sitting.

I continued to drink my Shandy (one of the perks of visiting the White Hart) and wondered how often Sam played the trick, possibly every day. I viewed him in a different light; obviously I had underestimated his intelligence. Sam raised his head and looked round at us for a moment, possibly his ears were burning, and then settled back to his doggy thoughts.

It certainly wasn't a dog's life for our Sam, 'the double crossing' dog.

Chapter 8   1967 I ONCE MET GRAHAM HILL

Aged 18

'Well I thought I'd have a stab at it.'

It was July of 1967 and I was eighteen-years-old. I had been lucky that summer, I had won a competition offered by the local education authority, and gained a place on the 'Junior Wings Scheme', which paid for me to have ten hours of flying lessons with the London School of Flying at Elstree Aerodrome just north of London. The airfield was small and only suitable for light aircraft. I was rather nervous about the prospect of buzzing around the sky in a small aeroplane, so had taken a summer holiday job at the airfield to get used to the idea. I was working as a 'bowser boy'; my job was to fill the petrol tanks of the aircraft as required. After some experimentation, I had found that my Isetta 300 bubble car would also run very satisfactorily on aviation spirit, and this was an added bonus. You would think that it would go much faster but it didn't. The light aircraft fuel was just normal petrol.

One late evening, it was quite dark, a couple of aircraft mechanics and I saw what we assumed was a plane several miles away in the sky, apparently lining up to land. It had no rotating red beacon on its tail, or red and green navigation lights on its wing tips, but the pilot was flashing its single headlight, and this was all that we could see. At this time, the landing lights down either side of the airstrip were switched off because no aircraft were expected at that late hour, and this was obviously what the pilot was trying to alert us to. As the control room staff had retired for an evening drink to the clubhouse bar before going home, there was nobody to answer any radio request from the pilot of the unscheduled plane.

The senior mechanic phoned the control tower, then the bar, and reported an unidentified flying object. The radio was quickly manned and the landing lights were switched on, but too late, the aircraft had already landed in the dark. We were all impressed.

The aircraft taxied off the landing strip, and into the parking area near the hangers. It stopped, the engines were switched off, and out of the left hand door alighted the pilot. He had a face and swept back haircut that were instantly recognisable: Graham Hill, the famous racing driver and TV personality. The chief mechanic pointed out the lack of rotation beacon on the tail plane, a bank note changed hands, and the bulb was quickly replaced. The red and green navigation lights were checked and found to be working but switched off. When asked about the difficulty of landing in the dark Mr Hill said, 'Well I thought I'd have a stab at it.'

Somebody asked him where he had been racing, and I am not sure where he said that he had come from but, apparently his Formula 1 car's suspension failed, and he had retired from the race and flown home; he was a very cool customer. He drove off home in his Lotus sports car, and that should be the end of the story.

During August and September of that year I started flying training with the London School of Flying and learned the arts of straight and level flight, circuits and bumps, spins and stalls and much more. My instructor, Pat Tree, seemed to enjoy my initial nervousness but was probably not really interested in teaching kids to fly when there were richer pickings to be had in the form of pop stars and actors from the nearby Elstree Film Studios. He was particularly annoyed that I constantly forgot to trim the aircraft, as we finished our climb after take-off. Trimming was accomplished by turning a handle mounted in the ceiling of the Piper Cherokee and made it easier to control the aircraft, eventually Mr Tree banged my hand hard against the handle and told me to, 'Trim the feckin thing.' He was Irish. I always remembered to do it after that because it had hurt. There are two well known training methods, the 'reward' method, and the 'punishment' method. Need I say more?

Our landing flight path took us over the rugby pitch of the Haberdashers School. In the airfield cafe, one lunchtime, another student came in from a training flight in a state of high excitement.

'What's the matter?' I asked.

'Oh,' he said, 'I brought my aircraft in so low over the rugby pitch that I think I managed to convert it.'

A cutting from 'The Times' about our course.

The Chief Instructor of the London School of Flying was an ex-RAF Spitfire pilot called Mr Higgins, who retained his handlebar moustache, and continued to use wartime RAF slang. Having a tea break was always preceded with, 'Right chaps, let's go and clean our swords.'

For my penultimate flight, Mr Higgins took charge. It had been Pat Tree on all my previous flights. We took the 'old girl' for a spin,' landed after the usual thirty mile circuit, and Mr Higgins got out, leaving me still in the left hand pilot's seat. Standing on the tarmac at the open door of the plane, he asked me if I had enjoyed my flights so far. I told him that I had.

'Well I hope that you enjoy this one,' he said, slamming the door and walking away.

I took the plane up and made my first solo flight. Obviously, it was a very memorable experience; I still have my logbook to prove that I did it. While I was flying at several thousand feet over Radlett, I remember looking uneasily at the empty instructor's seat next to me and thinking that the only person who was going to get me out of this situation and land the plane was me. This was probably the most important lesson that I learned on the course. I certainly never piloted a plane again.

Of course, if the necessity ever arose through both pilots falling ill on a commercial flight, I am sure that I would rise to the challenge. I mean, how hard can it be? They're all aeroplanes after all, two wings, a tail, a joystick, all that sort of thing. In later years, I had a go at hang gliding but felt that it was too risky. I tried normal gliding but it is difficult to make enough landings to be confident, when you cannot fly lots of 'circuits and bumps.' Worst of all was hot air ballooning, which consists of a pleasant launch, an unpredictable journey at the mercy of the wind, and a controlled crash landing unless the air is quite still.

Six years later, I was working as a mechanic in the Libyan oilfields and one evening, after work, I was sitting in the trailer of one Ronnie Boyle, quietly drinking his home brewed beer in the company of several other bored oil workers. This was before the Internet, DVDs, or even VCRs. Yes, we had to make our own entertainment, and mostly it came out of bottles. I told them the tale of Graham Hill and his daring feat. People nodded and reminisced about their own dodgy aircraft stories, usually bad landings on desert strips or bumpy rides in passenger airliners. Eventually the subject was exhausted and we found something else to talk about.

Some weeks later in November 1975 Ronnie came into my workshop. He had heard an announcement on the BBC World Service: Graham Hill had died in an air crash. He was killed when the light aircraft that he was piloting went down near Arkley golf course, while attempting a landing at Elstree Aerodrome at night, in foggy conditions. Five members of his Formula 1 team were also killed in the accident. Sadly, he had taken a second, but this time unsuccessful 'stab' at landing at Elstree in the dark.

It is ironic that, after all the calculated risks he had taken on the racetrack, it was on his way home that his luck ran out.

Chapter 9   1967 MY FIRST CAR WAS A BMW

Aged 18

While I was studying at Barnet College of Further Education in the 1960's, I became fed up with getting wet on two-wheeled transport, travelling between Barnet and my home in Borehamwood. Scooters were fine in the summer but they were unstable and uncomfortable in the winter, so I sold my Lambretta and bought myself a white, three-wheeled Isetta 300 bubble car. I named it 'Bucephalus' after Alexander the Great's horse.

Built by Bavarian Motor Works, ownership of this masterpiece of economic motoring was an epiphany for me. For the first time in my life I had a space that I could call my own. It was warm and dry and it is difficult to describe the feeling of well being I experienced just sitting in its tartan interior on our garage driveway, away from my parents and three brothers in our rather overcrowded end of terrace house on Whitehouse Avenue. This was my space and I could do what I liked in it. Usually, this involved nothing more exciting than the smoking of a quiet roll up, but occasionally I could persuade a member of the opposite gender to share it with me.

It was legal for me to drive my Isetta using my motorcycle license, as it was classified as a motorcycle and sidecar for the purposes of road tax. This meant that, eventually, I was able to take my car driving test after only one lesson, and to pass on the second attempt.

Isetta 300 - picture by Steve Glover

There is an urban myth that some bright spark always insists on recounting if you mention the Isetta 300, so I might as well bring it up for air now, before releasing it to sink down into the murky depths of the collective unconscious. Other makes of bubble car had doors on their sides but the Isetta's front end was hinged, with the steering wheel and control panel attached to it. The whole assembly opened outwards to allow access for the driver and passenger. In the early days the Isetta was supposedly manufactured without a reverse gear. The story goes that somebody built himself a very small garage for his bubble car and drove into it for the first time only to find that because the door was at the front of the vehicle, and it was up against the rear wall of the garage, he could neither get out of his car nor could he reverse due to the limitations of its gearbox. Apparently he stayed trapped until his wife noticed his absence and came and pulled the car back out of its shelter. This is obviously not a true story: most wives would have left him there.

Although it was supposed to accommodate only two people, I remember being four up in Bucephalus with me, my friend Adam, and two girls, puttering around North London at a somewhat reduced speed due to the overloading of the Isetta's motorcycle engine. We were packed in like sardines, what fun!

One of the problems with the model that I owned was its single rear wheel, which made it unstable when cornering. On one occasion, I was driving in rapid circles around the car park at Barnet College, trying to impress a female beauty therapy student with my driving prowess. As I recall, she was had not yet been won over to the prospect of being seen in my vehicle. A boyfriend with a sports car was her aspiration if not a sports car, then at least a car with four wheels. As she stood watching me doubtfully, my bubble car lost its balance due to its excessive cornering speed, and fell on its side, engine revving, wheels spinning. I scrambled out with some difficulty, having to climb under the door which was now top hinged due to the car's unusual position. Although I was able to quickly push my car back onto its three wheels, when I looked round, my prospect had come to a brisk decision and was nowhere to be seen.

Probably the most embarrassing incident for me, and one that does not show my 'so called friends' on our engineering course in a flattering light, was the occasion that my bubble car disappeared from the student car park. It was the end of the working day and I wanted to drive home. I searched and searched, but Bucephalus was nowhere to be found. I racked my brains and convinced myself that I had parked it on the residential street outside the college that morning. When I went to look, I found that somehow it was parked in the middle of somebody's front lawn. The problem was that the garden was surrounded by a low brick wall and there was only a pedestrian entrance. How could my car have ended up there? It was at this point that my 'friends' began to appear, smirking from around corners and behind cars, grinning at their cleverness and my perplexity. I recalled that it was my 'best friend' Adam who had manufactured an excuse to delay me from leaving at the end of our last lecture. The other six had scuttled out, picked up my chariot between them, and carried it into the garden. They took some persuading to pick it up again and carry it back out to the street. Although money did not actually change hands, cigarettes were handed out, phone numbers of beauty therapy students were revealed, and introductions to girlfriend's girlfriends were promised. There wasn't much else that boys of that age were interested in apart from food and I didn't have any of that.

I still see these people on our occasional reunions of the 'Class of 68.' They are all grown up now: grey haired, balding. Many of them have had successful careers, have raised families and gained the status of grandparents. They may look friendly and harmless but I know better; I haven't forgiven and I haven't forgotten.

Chapter 10   1967 THE DROWNING FARMER

Aged 18

It was in 1967 when I was eighteen that I went on my last family holiday with my mother, father and younger brother Nick. We stayed in a pension in Majorca, the food was good, the sea was warm, and there were three friendly and attractive girls of about our age staying. There was also a kidney shaped swimming pool surrounded by a tiled terrace. The hotel was on a rocky prominence about **twenty-five** metres above the sea, with a beach on one side and deep water on the other.

The three girls, me and my brother Nick

A couple of days after we arrived, we went to a 'Rustic Majorcan Evening.' This was a new experience for me at that time, although I know better now. The food was OK, the folk dancing was amusing, but the main interest for me was the bottles of rough red wine on our table. Nobody seemed to be drinking it, and I hated to see it go to waste. I had not previously been in a situation where there was no particular limit set on how much you could drink. I was very inexperienced with wine drinking. My parents were sitting on another table and therefore not watching me. They say that accidents happen when a combination of inopportune events occurs simultaneously, and in my case these were the inopportune events which led to my first unfortunate experience with the fruit of the vine.

My memory is of being shepherded to the toilets by my younger but more experienced brother. The 'whirling pits' plagued me as I lay in bed that night. My head was sore when I awoke next morning, and my brother Nick relished describing in detail my drunken behaviour on the bus back to the hotel. There were knowing looks at breakfast from the other guests who had been on the same trip.

'How are you feeling?' asked an 'old lady' of about fifty.

'Fine,' I said airily pretending to wonder why she bothered to ask. Even in those early days, I knew better than to admit to any pain or embarrassment the morning after.

'Never apologise, never explain,' said John Wayne, but under different circumstances I expect. My father was very nice about the whole thing, he probably saw it as a rite of passage for me, and I would love to be able to say that this one lapse had taught me a useful lesson. All I can say is that I wish that it had.

One of the waiters who served in the hotel restaurant was a medium sized fellow from South America. He was about thirty years old. I am not sure which country he came from but wherever it was, he had obviously lived on the coast and engaged in the sport of cliff diving. Every afternoon when he had a few hours off, he would appear in swimming trunks, on the hotel terrace, walk to the edge of the cliff, pause, stretch, pause again, and when he felt that he had the full attention of all the guests who were lying around the pool, he would dive off the cliff and plunge into the sea about fifty feet below. You had to be impressed. Well, I was, but my younger brother Nick felt that the man was showing off.

'I could do that,' he said. I pointed out that although he and I were excellent swimmers, having lived abroad for two years and **spending** most of our afternoons at a sports club swimming or surfing, we were not experienced at high diving. Nick was unrelenting and the next day saw him, in all his **trunk-wearing**, fourteen-year-old glory, standing on the cliff next to the waiter, about to take the plunge into the sea, and probably wishing that he had not actually voiced his opinion on the matter, in front of the girls. In all fairness, the waiter could not have been more helpful and encouraging. I climbed half way down the cliff so that I could jump in if Nick needed any help after his dive. Nick made the dive and although it was not technically perfect, his status on the terrace rose above the norm by about the same amount that mine had fallen the previous evening. Even I thought that he was a hero. We spent happy times at the pool, chatting to and not making any 'progress' with the three friendly, cheerful bikini clad English girls; they were very good company though.

Then, one day, the 'Young Farmers' arrived and everything changed. There were about ten couples, in their early twenties and all of them seemed to be well built people, both the males and the females. They made a lot of noise, ran around the pool, jumping in, making bombs and splashes, shouting, laughing, like excited barking Labradors chasing a ball; they were having a good time but were essentially harmless. Nick and I became quite friendly with them and as we were 'expert' swimmers in comparison to them, we kept our 'ends up' quite well, considering the age difference.

A couple of days after they had arrived, as I lay sun bathing, I noticed that one of the young farmers was teaching his fiancé to swim. He took her into the shallow end of the pool and held his arms out horizontally to support her, while she lay in them and splashed about, doing her best to swim. This happy scene went on for some time and my attention was diverted elsewhere. Foolishly, the fellow moved them slowly into the deep end and then chose this moment to let go of his partner and say,

'There, you're swimming, my love.'

The trouble was that she was not. Apparently, finding herself out of her depth and underwater her survival instincts kicked in, and she immediately grabbed hold of her instructor, threw her legs around his body trapping his arms at his sides. She pulled his face into her ample bosom, thus blocking his mouth and nose, and, gripping him with both arms, holding her head above the surface, proceeded to suffocate him, while using him as a float. He did not inhale any water, but he could not breathe or move except to kick his legs. She hung like this, in silent panic for some time; nobody noticed her situation, and slowly her helpless boyfriend lost consciousness, not that this affected his efficiency as a flotation device.

Eventually, somebody did notice; perhaps she screamed, I do not remember. Nick and I dived in and dragged the two of them to the side, where she made a tearful exit and disappeared from the scene. We pulled the boyfriend lifeless, floppy and unconscious from the pool and laid him on the tiles. It fell to me to attempt mouth to mouth resuscitation. Something I did not contemplate with any enthusiasm even though I had obtained a first aid qualification some years before, and was quiet proficient at the resuscitation of dummies. It all seemed very different in a real emergency situation. I stared down at the victim noting his grey, putty coloured skin, his blue lips, his immobility, and considered checking for loose dental work as recommended, when his eyelids suddenly flickered and opened. His colour came back in a rush and he took a huge breath, sat up and asked where his partner was. Thankfully, he had come back to life without me needing to intervene. He slowly got up and went in search of his partner, glad to be alive, but aware that he had made a huge mistake, and anxious to apologise to her.

What was the outcome of the incident? I do not know. Did they make up, forgive each other, marry and never speak of it again? We left for England soon after, as our holiday had ended.

There were several difficult lessons that I learned from this incident, the main one being that drowning people are very dangerous, and also that small mistakes can have big consequences.

Chapter 11   1969 PETE LOVE AND THE ANGEL OF DEATH

Aged 20

On one particular Saturday evening in the summer of 1969, 'Bob the driver,' Pete, Whit, Shram and I, all of us in our early twenties, were driving home from 'The Cat and Fiddle' in Radlett. As Bob was the proud owner of a reasonably new Mini car, he was particularly popular with his less affluent friends on a Saturday night.

We were on the way back to my rundown student flat above the 'Tan She Boutique' on Barnet High Street and decided to stop on the way for a quiet smoke. We agreed that a nice stopping place would be the top of Woodcock Hill, on the road between Elstree and Borehamwood. From this vantage point even Borehamwood looked good below us on a warm summer's evening, provided that you concentrated on the lights and ignored the distant derelict gas works. Pete and I had both been brought up in Borehamwood, and lived on the same street as kids. We shared happy memories of our little gang playing together on Woodcock Hill in summers past and sledging down it in the white winters of our childhoods. It was a familiar place for us.

As we sat smoking quietly, I told the company about a Dennis Wheatley novel that I was currently reading. At that time, Dennis Wheatley was very popular and his novel 'The Devil Rides Out' was a big hit with fans of the occult. Wheatley was considered to be an expert on this branch of things, and wrote with great authority on Satanism, black magic and the like. The other four 'heroes' pretended to be untroubled in the darkness but remember that truly frightening films, such as 'The Exorcist' were a thing of the future, and we had not yet been immunised against fear of the paranormal by overexposure to it.

I explained, with some relish and, I admit, a certain amount of dramatisation, the mechanics of summoning the Angel of Death from its hellish lair to set on your adversary, as described by Wheatley. Having risen from the depths, costumed in a suit of burnished silver armour, brandishing a sword and riding a large white stallion, it would capture your mortal enemy or even somebody with whom you mildly disagreed, and, holding them in an irresistible grip, drag them back down to Hell, to be subjected to eternal torture, anguish and humiliation. Its modus operandi was to turn to face its victim, and lifting the visor of its helmet, reveal the bony skull and fiery eyes beneath and, 'that's your lot mate,' down you go screaming in the inexorable express elevator to the scorching nether regions. Even your precious iPod would be taken from you, assuming that you had one. We didn't of course, they hadn't been invented yet.

Now, given access to an ally of this power, the perpetrator should be invincible but, like many seemingly desirable things, there was a catch. The fly in the supernatural ointment in this case was the fact that, if your opponent could ward off the Angel of Death, perhaps by carrying an amulet of the prescribed type a splinter of the true cross, a hermit's finger bone or the like then, having been frustrated, the supernatural horseman would turn on its erstwhile controller and, seizing him or her, drag them back down to Hades for the aforementioned treatment.

It was all very evocative on a dark and lonely hillside late at night, and the effect was somewhat amplified by the combined effects of the herbal cigarettes and the alcohol.

Unfortunately, and I knew this, Pete had a very low threshold for the supernatural. I really should not have been discussing the matter in his presence after dark. It was mischievous of me. But this was the late twentieth century and who in his right mind would believe in a load of old nonsense like that. Well, of course, in the hours of daylight, none of us. This wasn't daylight though.

Having listened to my narrative, unexpectedly, Pete decided to stand up and hop on one leg down Woodcock Hill with his arms outstretched like an aeroplane. He came back and insisted that he had discovered a new and wonderful experience, and that we should all share it by joining in. We were all far enough gone to think that this was a good idea and went along with it, hopping down the hill in a loose phalanx, arms outstretched like aeroplanes with Pete in the lead. We whooped with enjoyment as we took great hops down the hill in the starry darkness.

It was at this moment that a huge white horse rose up out of the ground six feet in front of Pete. It threw back its head and whinnied piercingly, rearing up on its hind legs and bicycling its front hooves in a terrifying manner. The rest of us were some yards behind Pete and were brought to a horrified, skidding, disordered halt. Pete was so close to the ghostly apparition that he almost crashed into it. I am surprised that he didn't fall instantly dead of heart failure. We all turned and ran back up the hill in a blind, chaotic, whimpering panic. Panting at the top, we frantically gathered our belongings, dived into the Mini, and with spinning wheels drove off towards the safety of civilisation. Well Barnet anyway.

Eventually, as we reviewed the situation, we gathered our composure, stopped panting and began to calm down. Bob unlocked his right leg and released his foot slightly from the accelerator. We began to realise that it had been, after all, only an ordinary horse. There was no armoured rider sitting on its back. We were not about to be dragged down to the fiery depths to be tormented by demons for eternity. Now I blame my naivety on my Catholic upbringing: I was preconditioned to believe in the supernatural in all its many unlikely forms. Pete, on the other hand, was supposedly a Baptist, so he really had no excuse. I am not sure about the religious proclivities of the other three.

Where did the white horse come from? Well, it had been tethered in the long grass on the hillside by its gipsy owner, who had thought that it would be safe there for the night. The horse had been innocently warning us that it didn't want a bunch of noisy, drunken youths falling all over it, ruining its repose and possibly injuring it.

Dejectedly, we drove back to my flat in Barnet, which was the first drop off point, and might have been the only one if the boys decided to stay for a coffee and to crash on my floor, as was usual on a Saturday night. I cannot remember whether they did or not - it was over forty years ago. I do remember that they roundly admonished me for telling ghost stories in inappropriate circumstances. So it was all my fault was it? Peer pressure forced me to sulkily agree to refrain from such behaviour on future outings. Secretly, however, as an inveterate storyteller, I felt that those had been the best of all possible circumstances for that particular story. I have never since been able to tell a story of any kind to such 'dreadfully' good effect, and I have told a few.

Later that year Bob crashed his mini while driving alone and too fast on a country road. As the car lay on its side in a ditch, wheels spinning, engine steaming, a concerned pedestrian ran up, and looking through the side window, saw that Bob was strapped in but not moving.

'He's dead,' he shouted fearfully up to his companion.

'No I facking ain't,' shouted Bob, 'get me aht of 'ere.'

Roger Ley

PART TWO YOUTH

Among the Djinns

Chapter 12   1969 THE STREAM OF FIRE

Aged 20

'Run for your life.'

I was a student apprentice, in the late sixties. I used to spend six months at Hatfield Polytechnic studying for a degree in engineering, and six months at the Engine builders Ruston and Hornsby in Lincoln. In one part of the large Ruston factory there was a shop floor toilet with an arrangement whereby a trough of continuously flowing water had toilet seats arranged in the top cover and low partitions between. Some of the apprentices found it hugely funny, when occupancy was high, to take a bundle of toilet paper, set it alight, and drop it into the upstream toilet. The flow of water would take it, flaming, along the length of the channel, before it was extinguished.

Apparently, you would see the occupants of the downstream cubicles yelp and stand up suddenly with loud exclamations of protest, their ruminations rudely interrupted - I cannot think of a more polite way of putting it. God help the unfortunate adolescent who was captured by one of the victims of his own scatological sense of humour. Drowning would be considered too good for him.

Things were no better in the urinals where the all-metal construction offered the opportunity for an apprentice to connect a 'megger tester' to the pipe work using a crocodile clip. Rapidly rotating the handle of the device caused a very high voltage to be generated, albeit at low current, rather like an electric fence. Certain sphincter muscles within the bodies of any unfortunate victims standing using the urinals would contract, flow would cease, and the circuit would be broken. The muscle would relax, flow would immediately resume, the circuit would be remade and the process would repeat itself until the victim regained some control of their output and could turn on the comedian who was the cause of their discomfiture. There would be a moment's grace while clothing was adjusted, but then – Run apprentice, run for your very life.

Chapter 13   1974 I START WORKING IN THE OILFIELDS

Aged 25

'You'll never guess what this bloke just said.'

I graduated from Hatfield Polytechnic in 1972, finished my industrial training at Ruston and Hornsby, and accepted a job as a Junior Research Engineer. Ruston's was a big engine builder in Lincoln and the major employer in the city.

At just about the same time my father died suddenly from a massive heart attack; he was only fifty-two years old. His death had a profound effect on me. For years he had been keen that at least one of his four sons should go to university and get a degree, and he coached all four of us so that we passed the eleven plus exam and found places at Grammar schools. Although I had not gone to a university, I had still gained a degree, the first one in our family to do so, and I sent him a copy of my notification, so he knew that I had passed the exams but unfortunately he died before he could attend the graduation ceremony some months later. My mother and brother Nick did come, but I was disappointed that he was not there to celebrate my achievement. In fact, his early death meant that he could never be present at any of the important events in my later life, and I felt his loss deeply at such times.

I think that I was unsettled by the suddenness and finality of my father's death, and the whole idea of a safe, steady job seemed less important. At about this time the girl that I had been seeing and wanted to marry, decided that she liked somebody else more than me. As she lived next door, and I didn't want to keep bumping into her with her new beau, I decided to move to a different part of the city and broke contact with my housemates.

After about a year I found that working as a research engineer was not really 'rocking my boat.' It was just too ordinary going in to work at the same desk every working day. In desperation, I applied to the National Aeronautics and Space Administration in the USA for astronaut training. This was during the time that the USA was regularly sending men to the Moon. NASA immediately turned me down, of course. I was in no way qualified to be an astronaut with ten hours of flying experience and a thoroughly pedestrian degree in mechanical engineering.

Happily, I bumped into an ex-flatmate in the Adam & Eve pub in Lincoln, and he told me that he was working as a gas turbine mechanic in Libya and, more importantly, what he was earning; I could not believe it. It would be meaningless to give a figure now, suffice it to say that at Ruston's as a research engineer with a degree and full industrial training, I had been earning about a quarter of this, and he did not even have to pay income tax. Before I knew it, a week or so later, I was landing at Tripoli airport having been recruited by an employment agency in Gt Yarmouth who had found me a job as a turbine mechanic at Zueitina oil terminal on the coast of the Libyan Desert.

In fact, I knew about as much about gas turbines as I did about calligraphy, but I flew out to Triploi almost penniless and made my way to the hotel near to the offices of 'Oilfield Imports of Libya', who were the contracting company that I was going to work for. Given that the Internet was a long way from being invented, along with DVDs and hand held computers, there wasn't much to do. Locally, the first language was Arabic and the second was Italian, so there were no books or magazines on sale that I could read. Libya was and still is a 'dry' country, so when I ate in the hotel the wine waiter would come over with a napkin over his arm in the prescribed fashion and offer me Coke, Fanta or 7 up. It was quite bizarre.

There was another expatriate called Pete Lansdown staying at the hotel. He was also being sent to Zueitina terminal. He became a good friend for the next two years and a big help with my transition to the way of life I would lead in Libya. An ex-merchant navy engineer, he put me straight on various issues, rather like an older brother. Eventually, Pete and I flew out together to the desert strip at Zueitina terminal in a Fokker Friendship aircraft, 'the little Fokker' as it was affectionately known.

Mike Norris, who was to be our senior foreman, met us off the plane. Now 'Mr Mike' as he was known by the Libyans, was the epitome of a desert oilman: he was tanned, taciturn, had sun bleached blonde hair, wore khaki shorts and the sleeves torn out of his khaki shirt - he looked like a genuine hero. I could not wait to tear the sleeves out of my shirt, too, although my scrawny, white arms would not really look the same. I decided to wait until I had 'got my knees brown', as they used to say in the British Army. He drove us from the airstrip in his Toyota Land cruiser, and we were allocated accommodation in the trailer park. After this, he took us to the main site to see the gas turbines that we were to maintain. They produced all the electricity for the terminal.

As Mike, Pete and I looked at the seven large machines, I became aware that the sand filtration ducting at the front end was largely indistinguishable from the exhaust ducting at the other. Before I could stop, I heard myself saying, 'But which is the front and which is the back?'

Mike gulped, did a double take and then roared with laughter, thinking that I was joking. Pete knew the truth and said nothing, but gave me an old fashioned look. Anyway, the ice was broken and Mike said, 'You'll do OK here with a sense of humour like that.' Then he clapped me on the shoulder and took us into the workshop. 'You'll never guess what this bloke just said,' he chuckled as he introduced me to the other turbine mechanics. 'We were worried that you might be some chancer, who didn't know anything about turbines as nobody from Ruston's had heard of you.'

My question had been serious if mistimed, but I laughed knowingly along with the rest of the mechanics; at least I had the sense not to compound the mistake.

The author next to one of the three turbo pumps at Zueitina

In the meantime, I had fulfilled a boyhood

dream; I was now officially a 'desert man', working in the North African oilfields on a very high wage. Things were looking up!

We worked in the desert for thirty-three days at a time, and flew back to the UK for twenty-one days off. This was our '33/21' field break schedule. One of my friends was always seen off at the airport in Middlesbrough by his wife and small son, and they were always there to greet him when he got back. He told me that on one occasion, as the little boy was waving the aeroplane off, he turned to his mother and asked, 'But what does daddy do on the aeroplane for thirty-three days?'

Chapter 14 1975 ARRESTED AT TRIPOLI AIRPORT

Aged 26

'They're dying to shoot one of us.'

Working in the oilfields involved making many sacrifices. The most obvious one was the lack of female company, particularly difficult if, like me, you were in your mid-twenties at the time. Next on the list should have been the prohibition of alcohol. As mentioned before, Libya is a 'dry' country, but this last problem was solved by our own manufacture on site of gallons of beer and quantities of Vodka or 'Flash', as we called it. We also had a powerful craving for pork in all its various forms. If the Libyan customs people found you carrying any foodstuff into the country they would confiscate it and, of course, pork is not allowed in the diet of any Muslim, so it never appeared on the menu in our mess hall.

My way around all this difficulty was to make use of what was already available. The fashion at that time for tall boots and flared jeans; if you have rather slender calf muscles like me, there was plenty of room in the boots for two packs of bacon, a half bottle of whiskey and a couple of magazines, all of which would make the next month's stay in the desert a little more bearable. On one occasion, a fellow worker, the site chemist, invited some of us round to his room to share a small pork pie that he had managed to smuggle through customs. We each got a tiny piece, but it was a fine experience. I closed my eyes and was transported back to England for a Sunday lunchtime pint in the garden of my local pub.

Getting in and particularly out of Libya, was a

nightmare of the first order, and I have never experienced anything comparable at any airport elsewhere. The operative word is 'queuing,' and the Libyans at that time had no concept of it. In Tripoli airport, the departure hall had four small windows at the far end, at one of which you had to present your passport to be stamped before you could get on the plane to go home. Between the entrance and the windows was a mêlée rather reminiscent of an upright Rugby scrum, with about two hundred players. I have seen men faint in the heat and crush, and have to be dragged out of it. On one occasion, I remember finally getting onto a Caledonian Airways flight, after struggling for two hours in the 'Turkish bath' of the passport control area. My clothes were soaked with sweat, and I was trembling with a combination of exhaustion, stress and dehydration. I looked as if I had been under a shower. The air stewardess pointed out that I was late and had delayed the takeoff but then, she had never bothered to debark when the plane landed at Tripoli and didn't know what conditions were like in the departure area. She went and got me a pint of water and some salt when I asked her to, and became quite considerate when I explained the difficulties involved in embarkation. I used to feel such relief as the plane left the ground and soon afterwards left Libyan airspace, a relief of a magnitude seldom experienced by other travellers. I felt as if I was being released from prison; the pleasure was enhanced by the taste of the first glass of real beer and a feeling of returning to civilisation.

    Some of my workmates used to open a bottle of coke before leaving the oil terminal, pour three-quarters of it away and fill it back up with homemade Vodka, then recap it. They could then calmly sit around the airport getting a buzz on. I do not know if this would have helped or not. In fact oil workers had a bad reputation for drunkenness on these flights home. I knew two oil workers who were put off their homeward flight for rowdy behaviour. The plane made an unscheduled stop at Rome airport, and the delinquents found themselves stepping off the plane and into the arms of the local police.

My worst experience of transit through Tripoli was thanks to a stout electrician from Middlesbrough called Colin McCann, who was my trailer mate back at Zueitina. Colin had decided to buy a bottle of duty-free whisky at Heathrow airport, after consuming several pints of beer, and to drink three-quarters of it on the flight to Tripoli. Colin was drunk and when we entered Libyan airspace, the chief steward on our Libyan Arab Airlines flight approached him and politely explained that it was now illegal for him to be in possession of alcohol, and offered to dispose of the bottle. Colin was abusive in his reply and refused to give up the whisky. The steward withdrew without a word, and a few minutes later, after we landed, and as Colin was walking down the aircraft steps, four plain-clothed policemen arrested him. This was not a good thing, and I was at pains to explain to him that he must be calm and not hit anybody because that would make things ten times worse. He was a bit of a rough diamond. The police took him away but, as he had given the whisky bottle to somebody else on the flight, they had no evidence, so the next thing that they did was to arrest the people in the seats on either side of him. That would be me and another electrician called Bob: most electricians are called Bob in my experience. We were handcuffed and driven away to a police station. I would like to mention at this point that I had consumed no alcohol that day. It was always my policy to arrive and depart from Tripoli stone cold sober; life is complicated enough when dealing with Libyan customs, immigration and security police, all of whom carry guns, without adding alcohol to the mix.

In the police station, a rather bored policeman questioned us and slowly wrote a report. Our problem was that the interview was being conducted and recorded in Arabic, and there was no translator present. We had no idea what was happening, where we would be going, and we all dreaded that we might be separated and put in different cells with local criminals. Basically, it was not a good experience. We were escorted to a clinic where an English speaking Pakistani doctor pronounced Colin and Bob to be drunk and me to be sober. The test for sobriety was to stand on one leg with your eyes closed and your arms outstretched. Funnily enough, just the same pose that Pete Love had espoused on Woodcock Hill some years before. Try it, and then try it again having drunk a pint of beer. I just did and cannot do it sober, now at the age of sixty-six, but I could at the age of twenty-five.

As we sat in the waiting room of the police station with uniformed men walking past us carrying guns of all shapes and sizes, and all talking loudly in Arabic, one side of Bob's handcuffs fell open. I leaned close and whispered in his ear, 'They're dying to shoot one of us.'

He blanched, quickly closed the misbehaving cuff, and nervously held it closed with the other hand until later, when they removed it.

I must say that we were never mistreated, although I have never slept on a more stained or unhygienic looking mattress. All human life was there and probably a lot of other species. We were released the next day into the arms of our blessed maintenance supervisor, who had come to retrieve us and take us back to Zueitina terminal, where Colin was given a talking to by the terminal Superintendent: when you work in a foreign country you must obey the local laws. One should be extra careful when the dictator, who is running the country, is as dangerous and ungovernable as Colonel Gadaffi.

Colin and Bob had been charged with drunkenness, and I had been released without charge. A month later Bob went home on field break and never returned. Typically, Colin fronted it out, went to court two months later, and, after a lot of incomprehensible arguing between his lawyer and the judge, was fined a dinar - about a pound sterling.

The government did not want to bother the expats unduly, as long as we didn't give booze to any Muslim workers. They just wanted us to pump the oil out.

The best-paid people on the site were the 'mooring masters.' These were ship's captains who were paid to sit around doing very little, and occasionally would be taken out in a launch to pilot an oil tanker up to the loading buoys, where the tanker would be connected to the terminal with large flexible hoses so that crude oil could be pumped into them. Pink gins all round in the tanker captain's stateroom. Probably the stupidest thing that I saw one of them, a Scot, do, was to try to smuggle a set of stolen tools through customs on the way out of Tripoli airport. The customs official had the captain's bag open, and the captain was trying to explain what the tools were doing in there. It made me realise that some people will still pilfer even when they are very well paid and have no need. It seems to be hard wired into them; perhaps it depends on your upbringing.

Chapter 15   1975 NICK POOLE'S NICE PINK PARTY FROCK

Aged 26

'June is busting out all over.'

One of the mechanics that I worked with at Zueitina Terminal, actually probably the best turbine mechanic on the site, was Nick Poole. He always wore shorts, boots, a pair of mirrored sunglasses, a floppy khaki hat, and he had a full beard.

Nick Poole and myself working on a turbo pump

On the day in question, we were working together in the workshop attached to the main turbine sets, probably rebuilding fuel pumps.

Anyway, Nick was looking through the rag pile (we used to have bales of them delivered regularly), and what should he find but a lovely pink cotton dress that was just his size. He put it on over his shorts, hat, and sunglasses and it fitted him 'perfectly'. He was not a tall man and the dress came halfway down his shins. He looked like a singularly unconvincing cross-dresser, with his safety boots and his beard. Quite honestly, in the workshop setting, he looked surreal.

Anyway, everybody liked Nick in the pink dress. Boredom was a big problem on site; we were there for a month at a time, working seven days a week, with very little in the way of entertainment. This was before the days of the Internet, DVDs or even video recorders. All we had after work were books and homemade beer. At tea break the Libyan mechanics, Mufta and Ibrahim, liked the dress, the other 'Inglesi' mechanics liked the dress; it was all a big laugh and then, after many jokes, comments and suggestions, we all got back to work.

At this point, onto the scene comes the 'Big Mudiir'. 'Mudiir' is the Arabic word for manager or boss. I had raised a laugh one day with the Libyan mechanics who could not speak much English, by describing myself as a 'mini-mudiir.' They knew what 'mini' meant for some reason. Probably from 'mini-skirt', a word that had penetrated even to the Magreb by 1975.

Anyway, the Mudiir in question was a visiting senior manager from our parent oil company in America, Occidental Petroleum of California, usually referred to as 'Oxy'. The visitor was a big man and, as he was a field man, he was used to American blue-collar types, known as 'rough necks' in the oil fields. They usually portrayed themselves as big, taciturn, manly, hard drinkin', tattooed and preferably Texan. The visiting manager was escorted by the Terminal Superintendent into our rest area next to the workshop, to be introduced to our senior foreman, Mike Norris, an ex-RAF Chief Technician who was very calm and good in an emergency. As they were shaking hands, Nick, not knowing of the visiting senior manager, carrying a large spanner, wearing his hat, sunglasses, beard, and pink dress walked nonchalantly past the open doorway singing very loudly, 'June is busting out all over.' We always sang loudly because we liked the acoustics in the workshop and it helped to break up the boredom. There was an awkward pause.

'Who the f*** was that?' asked the American manager, clearly shocked rigid and probably wondering if he was hallucinating.

'That was Nick Poole, one of our best turbine mechanics,' said Mike declining to develop his explanation,and managing to give the impression that nothing unusual had happened.

'He needs to go on field break,' said the manager shaking his head and pondering the cultural differences between the Limeys and the Yanks. Apparently, Americans find pantomime difficult to understand, what with women dressed as men, men dressed as women, dames, principal boys, ugly sisters and what not. Anyway, nothing more was said and the Mudiir's tour of the terminal continued. Soon afterwards, we were awarded a significant pay rise, but there may have been no connection.

Chapter 16   1975 WALLY THE WELDER'S POORLY BAD FOOT

Aged 26

'I'm not sending you home early, Wally.'

There were two doctors at Zueitina terminal. One was a young Egyptian eye specialist who was using his expat earnings to set up an eye clinic back home in Egypt. The other was an older man, a Maltese, who had problems with cataracts. There were a couple of indicators of his poor sight. One was the wig he wore which had not gone grey, while the natural hair below it had. The other clue was that in the mess hall he held the menu (such as it was) up to his right eye and about five centimetres from it in order to make his choices. This did not inspire confidence in his diagnostic abilities amongst the expat contingent on the site.

One of the few American mechanics on site was Dick Fourier. Dick worked in the heavy vehicle workshop and if he came over to the maintenance workshop for something, he would always take his leave with a casual, 'Ma salama mother f*****.' 'Ma salama' is Arabic for goodbye or literally, 'Go in peace.' One day, Dick went to the older doc with something in his eye and the good doctor dripped in the wrong preparation, so that the pupil was fully dilated, which is not a comfortable thing in very bright sunlight. He had meant to put in a green dye, which helped to highlight damage to the cornea.

'Oh well, Dick,' said the doc, nonchalantly, while peering myopically at the label on the bottle, 'if you can't see, don't drive.'

This was symptomatic of his somewhat casual

approach to our medical care.

The medical case that most significantly highlighted this approach concerned Wally the welder's foot. Wally was a cheerful Geordie welder who had a lot of curly black hair, a big moustache, bushy sideburns and a very red face. The Libyan welders, who worked with him and had learned some English from him, had also acquired a very interesting accent, which combined their North African with Wally's Geordie. It sometimes made communication difficult if Wally sent one of them from the marine section where he worked, to our maintenance workshop with a message.

'We divn't na what ta di,' for example, which translates as 'We don't know what to do.'

One morning Wally was standing, welding on a large buoy, which was floating in the harbour. One of the marine section tugs had taken him out there. Wally did not notice that the mooring cable, which attached the boat to the buoy, was lying over his foot. As the boat drifted and the cable tightened, Wally called out in distress but his foot was a bit crushed before the crew could start the tug's engine and move forward to release the tension in the cable. He actually fell into the water and a couple of the divers, who were on the tug, dived into the sea and rescued him.

Wally was taken limping to the doctor, who couldn't see much wrong with the foot. This was hardly surprising since he couldn't see much of anything. He dismissed Wally from the surgery with a bottle of paracetamol. A day or so later, Wally's foot had gone blue, and when it was presented to the doctor, he sent Wally away again with the accusation.

'You're swinging the lead, Wally. I'm not sending you home early.'

A couple of days passed and the foot had

swollen to twice its normal size and was going black. The doctor said, 'If you want a crutch, have a crutch,' and impatiently passed him one out of the medical cupboard.

I was walking into the mess at the same time as the doc the next day. Wally was there, leaning against the wall adjusting the crutch, with his big black foot on display. On seeing him the doc leaned towards me and said, 'I prescribed him a parrot, but it flew away,' and continued into the mess chuckling at his own fulsome wit. The rest of us were pretty appalled - we wondered what it would take to be sent home sick.

In the end, the terminal superintendent intervened and sent Wally home, much to the doctor's chagrin. Some weeks later, Wally returned, having had the foot repaired back in the UK.

'How's the foot Wally?' asked the doc when he bumped into him.

'Oh,' said Wally, 'they X-rayed it at the hospital in Newcastle, and there was a bone broken. I cannot bend it the same as I used to be able to.' He demonstrated the difference in flexibility between his left and right feet.

'Ah Wally,' said the doc 'you're a welder, not a f****** ballet dancer.'

And that was the end of that.

Chapter 17   1975 THE WRECK OF THE FRANCIS HOLMES

Aged 26

This next section has some technical content which may not be of interest to some readers. It is a very important section to me though, because it describes a bad accident in which I was involved and brought home to me how dangerous our work could be. You could argue that we were in as much danger as soldiers in a war. The difference was that we did not have the British Army to back us up and fly us home in the event of injury or accident. We were on our own. I have never been able to forget the explosion on the Francis Holmes and the six men who died, nor have I forgotten how avoidable the accident was, and that it was caused by one moment of inattention.

Zueitina oil and gas terminal is on the North African coast and, at the time that I worked there, it consisted of an oil pumping terminal, a gas plant and a marine department which was based at the end of a long jetty. The purpose of the terminal was to load oil and gas onto tankers. These tankers could not come close to shore as there was no harbour or deep water, so they were anchored to large buoys off-shore, there to swing on their moorings depending on the wind and tide. The buoys were anchored to the seabed and connected to the underwater pipelines that took the oil and gas to them. For loading, the tankers were connected to the pipelines by large floating flexible hoses, and it was the job of the marine department to make these connections when a tanker arrived. The tankers were piloted up to the buoys by one of our team of 'mooring masters', who were all qualified ships captains.

In order to get the large, heavy flexible hoses connected between the buoys and the tankers, there was a work boat called the 'Francis Holmes' which was equipped with a crane and was crewed by a mix of about a dozen Maltese and British divers and mechanics. One day, they had hoisted a flexible hose onto the front deck of the Francis Holmes, and were trying to split one of the couplings between two sections. One of the inch diameter bolts would not come undone and, because all the others had been removed, there was a considerable spillage of a quite volatile type of crude oil over the deck of the ship. The oil flowed through gaps in a wooden hatch cover and flooded into a section of the hold. This was a very dangerous situation with hundreds of gallons of oil spilling around and giving off a flammable gas.

At this point, unbelievably, one of the crew lit a gas-cutting torch to cut through the remaining bolt. The chief engineer shouted from the bridge 'Put that torch o--'

Just as the gas in the hold ignited and the resulting explosion blew the hatch cover to pieces, killed six men outright and burned many others including the captain and chief engineer who also suffered cuts from the windows of the bridge as they were blown in.

I was working on shore as usual, and the first I knew about it was when the chief electrician pointed the ship out on the horizon. It looked like an atomic explosion, a perfect mushroom cloud with the Francis Holmes at the base. I had not heard the explosion over the noise of the turbines that I was working on.

All worked stopped on the terminal and all available men went by truck to the marine department with a view to saving the crew and possibly putting the fire out. Tugboats were dispatched, but there was little to be done except load up the body bags and bring the dead and injured back to the camp. People were patched up and sent to the local hospital in the town of Ajedabia or shipped home to Malta or the UK. A slightly disturbing aspect of the accident was the speed with which our stores, which never usually had anything that you wanted in stock, were able to issue six shiny, new, insulated, aluminium coffins.

The ship stayed where it was floating in the bay anchored by the heavy flexible hose draped over its prow and she burned for days. We found two other bodies floating in the sea on the day of the explosion, and the last two washed ashore about a week later. A couple of days after the explosion two mechanics agreed to go abroad the stricken ship to load the two blackened bodies that were still lying on the deck into body bags. Sometime later, I asked one of them how he felt about it and he said that he was still having nightmares.

Months later, the ship broke free during a storm and an onshore wind drove her onto the beach. I went to look at her about a year after the accident and the ubiquitous sand blowing across the desert had filled her up through her now open hatch covers, and that will be her final resting place. Forty years later, the Francis Holmes still lies partially buried on the beach at Zueitina, now a rusted hulk, her story forgotten. I can find no mention of it on the Internet except for the two pages from the 'Times of Malta', which I have included in the appendices.

The wreck of the Francis Holmes forty years later

The Oil Company hired another work boat from Holland, called 'the Crab', and things carried on much as before.

The Dutch crew of the Crab soon settled into the job. I got the impression that if they had not been legally employed by Occidental, they would have reverted to their normal job as pirates. They had a fascination for all things made of brass and had a huge bundle of scrap brass dangling on a heavy cable underneath the ship where the police and customs could not see it. No doubt, they eventually took it back to Holland to sell it. I knew about this because I was later given some scuba diving lessons by one of the divers from the Crab, and I used to swim past it. Out of politeness, I never mentioned it to him

During one of these lessons, I swam alone down to the seabed beneath the ship, about twenty feet below the surface, to investigate some pieces of rope that were drifting around down there. As I got closer I suddenly realised that the 'ropes' were a pair of Moray eels. Each about a metre and a half long, they were twined closely together and as they saw me, their heads moved in unison to track me. I was very scared and made hurriedly for the surface making as much noise and turbulence as possible. Fortunately, they did not follow me. Moray eels are big, ugly, aggressive and bad-tempered creatures. I can say this about them because I am on dry land and they cannot get to me here, but they are a species that is best left alone.

Scuba diving from the 'Crab,' I am on the right.

Chapter 18   1975 THE BAR AT ZUEITINA TERMINAL

Aged 26

The barbecue went off like a bomb

As I have mentioned before, Libya is a dry country and alcohol is completely banned, so why was it that we had a fully equipped bar and recreation club? The reason was, that both the Oilfield Police and the Secret Police could not see it, and why couldn't they see it? Well, because they had been told that they could not see it by their superiors, who knew that it would be very difficult to recruit expats if they could not have a beer now and then. I should mention that we knew that there were Secret Police stationed nearby because they had a camp a couple of kilometres away. Outside this camp was a large notice which said 'Secret Police Camp' in large red letters in both Arabic and English. I always found this rather pleasantly ironic.

Our recreation club had been formed by connecting a number of trailers together. We had a decent sized room with a bar, which served homemade beer and homemade vodka. This was manned on a voluntary basis by ourselves and was open three days a week. We had a television room but could receive only Arabic stations, a poolroom with a pool table, a snooker room with a full sized snooker table and a small library. On Fridays, we had a barbecue, and the divers from the Francis Holmes, or later the Crab, would come with fish that they had speared. The mess would donate steaks, and Dick Fourier would make his famous American mofo barbecue sauce. The first time that I went to one of these soirees I was introduced to somebody that I didn't know and, to make conversation, I asked him if he was a diver.

'Yes, I'm a muff diver,' he informed me, and I was so green that I didn't know what he meant and asked him if he needed any special equipment to practice this occupation. I will not trouble you, dear reader, with his reply.

One Friday afternoon soon after I had arrived in Libya, Mike Norris sent me back to the trailer park from the maintenance workshop an hour early with a bottle of barbecue starter liquid and instructions to 'light her up' so that it would be ready for cooking at about six o'clock. I tipped about a litre of the liquid over the charcoal, it was a big barbecue and before I lit it, I took the precaution of stepping back and throwing some burning paper at it. It was a fortunate move because the liquid in question was something called 'C5' which is very volatile and the barbecue went off like a bomb.

We mechanics were issued with only one set of overalls which we would sometimes wash in a bucket of C5 just before lunchtime and leave them hanging over a fence so that they would be dry when we came back to work. One of the electricians came back from his lunch break early one afternoon, and having put on his slightly damp overalls, lit up a cigarette. He was immediately surrounded by a thin corona of flame and after a moment's hesitation found it suddenly necessary to remove his overalls faster than I have ever seen anybody remove any item of clothing before, let alone a full set of awkwardly restrictive overalls.

It is worth describing how we manufactured alcohol for the bar and indeed for our own private use. The making of homemade beer hardly needs explaining, but Flash was a different matter. For beer production, we would bring back tins of malt extract and packets of yeast. With the help of a large bucket and a few other items of equipment, it was possible to make a passable beer. Occidental actually issued us with a kilogram of malt extract each month as a 'dietary supplement.'

'There's no bad beer, just some is better than others,' went the saying, until one of the crew brought back a tin of malt extract with added cod liver oil that he had bought at Boots. We called the resulting beverage 'Fish beer,' and still drank it but with less than our normal enthusiasm.

The biggest danger was that we could not get hold of bottles made from tempered glass, which could resist the pressure that built up after the beer had been bottled. We used to use one litre milk bottles, and if the pressure built up too much, they would explode with fearsome consequences, although it must be said that thankfully, I never saw one blow up in anybody's hand but I saw some brewing cupboards with glass embedded in their insides.

The making of vodka was a whole different ball game. As soon as I arrived on site I was issued with a six-page document called 'The Blue Flame.' The oil companies quietly published this in the hope of preventing accidental explosions on their sites. Boiling a bucket of alcohol is rather like boiling a bucket of petrol. They are both very flammable and very bad accidents will happen. One day, soon after I arrived, the doctor rushed around the camp asking people if they knew their blood type and taking them back to the surgery to make donations for a mechanic in another camp. His still had overheated and blown up after he had fallen asleep sitting with it bubbling in his trailer. The explosion blew the trailer to pieces. As the mechanic was wearing only a pair of shorts and boots he suffered seventy per cent burns. They flew him the UK, but he could not be saved.

He died about two weeks later.

I believe that distilling alcohol in the oilfields of Saudi Arabia and North Africa originated from the employment of Americans with their history of prohibition in the nineteen thirties. The clue that somebody is running a still is their need to acquire large quantities of white sugar, which is the raw material for fermentation. We had a site still about as big as a dustbin, which stayed in the distillation room of the bar and was run very carefully by the maintenance crew. The Libyan authorities ignored all our involvement with alcohol as long as we did not give any to Muslims. This could be difficult at times as the Palestinian mechanics that we worked with could be quite insistent. They wanted a beer but did not dare make any as the Libyans would see this as a serious crime, because they were fellow Muslims, and they would be deported or worse.

There was altogether far too much alcohol available on the site. Some of the guys had to go back to their trailers for a 'livener' in the mornings. One of my friends even managed to drive a Land Cruiser into a thirty-inch oil pipeline while drunk one night. He found himself on the next plane home in the morning, and was never heard from again. Oil Companies do not tolerate the risk of an interruption to the flow of oil (their revenue) even for sound reasons such as routine maintenance let alone stupid, drunken behaviour.

On the subject of self-indulgence, the Gas Plant Superintendent was a rotund, crew-cut American who had a concession-sized ice cream machine in his office, and would generously offer a bowl to visitors, probably because it gave him the excuse to further indulge himself. For no good reason that I ever heard expressed, it was rumoured that he was reporting back to the CIA. Almost certainly some of us expats had some connection with their home secret services British, American, Palestinian, Egyptian and the like. Zueitina terminal was a very important part of the Libyan economy and would definitely have been of military interest, given Libya's backing of various terrorist groups. At that time, both the IRA and the Loyalist paramilitaries had separate training camps in different parts of the Libyan desert, both were sponsored by Colonel Gaddafi who was happy to give backing to anybody who would cause trouble to the British government. Allegedly, during the Cold War, British merchant mariners sold photographs of Iron Curtain port installations and the like to the British Secret Service. They gathered the photographs through a postal operation.

There were many risks associated with working in the desert apart from sunburn and dehydration. Out of sheer boredom, one of the instrument mechanics and I used to go snake hunting under the rocks around the camp and caught Horned Vipers, a very dangerous occupation I now realise. Scorpions were also greatly prized and the largest were collected, humanely killed in alcohol and mounted in clear, liquid plastic, then hardened to form blocks. These were taken back to the UK as trophies. We always tapped out our boots or protective gloves before putting them on, for fear that a scorpion had made a home of one of them. The doctor told me that scorpion and snake bites tend usually to be on the hand or foot, either through the beasties being in boots or because the casualty had reached into a dark space under a bed or in a dark corner.

Another risk was the local packs of wild dogs, which might or might not be rabid. There was always some fool who started feeding them and encouraging them to come into the trailer camp, until one day a mooring master was nipped by a puppy and the doctor insisted on giving him a series of very unpleasant injections with unusually long needles. The army was called in and the wild dogs were culled.

Chapter 19   1976 INSIDE THE ENGINE AND THE DESERT DJINN

Aged 26

Testosterone has a lot to answer for

As I have mentioned before, my main duty was as part of the team tending the ten Ruston TA gas turbines on the site. One day, it became apparent that one of them had a badly misaligned burner. This meant that the flame in the combustion chamber fired to one side and not down the centre, so there was a risk of heat damage to the wall of the chamber. I am well aware that very few of my readers will be interested in the detailed technicalities so I will be as brief as is possible. The TA has an external combustion chamber somewhat larger than two dustbins placed end to end. At one end is the burner assembly, which is easily removed, but to align it correctly, the whole combustion chamber has to be removed so that it can be observed from the upstream end. So there we were, Mike Norris our senior foreman, Pete Lansdown, Colin Blowers, Nick Poole and myself, discussing the week it would take to accomplish the task, working in the hot sun (it being August) and how we would proceed with it. The engine was part of the power generation system for the oil terminal and Occidental would want it back on line as quickly as possible. We would have to work, in shifts, around the clock and there was also the question of heavy lifting gear to be considered.

Ever the lateral thinker, I heard myself say, 'If we just took the burner assembly off and somebody crawled backwards inside the combustion chamber we could put the assembly back on, bolt it up and adjust it while the man inside the engine could direct the positioning by talking through one of the sighting holes.' In the picture below, the combustion chamber is in the foreground.

There was a pause while everybody thought about what a good idea this was and what a lot of work it would save but how nobody would be stupid enough to put themselves in such an unpleasant position, actually bolted inside the combustion chamber of an industrial gas turbine engine. Surely, nobody would be daft enough to do that! Suddenly I heard a voice say, 'I'll do it,' and to my horror I realised that the voice was my own. Testosterone has a lot to answer for I always think.

Ruston TA1500 gas turbine with the combustion chamber at the front
Picture courtesy of Siemens

It was eventually agreed that this was exactly what we would do. Permissions were given, precautions were taken, I even found myself disconnecting the starter batteries, threatening various people with dire consequences if any 'funny' tricks were played, and before you know it there I was bolted inside the engine with only a torch for comfort. The guys working on the outside made the adjustments and then there seemed to be a long pause when nothing happened and nobody spoke to me through the sight hole. I banged on the inside of the chamber to attract attention. Why were they not letting me out? I wanted to know? I banged again harder and the torch went out leaving me in total darkness while my friends worked outside in what seemed to me to be a glacially slow pace. Time seemed to stretch. Eventually, I was released from my incarceration, nobody was playing tricks, it had just taken a little time. The Welsh safety officer patted me on the back.

'Well done boyo,' he said, 'you've saved a lot of work for yourselves there.'

I had never suffered from claustrophobia before but ever since this incident I have had an aversion to confinement in spaces that I cannot escape from easily, such as the rear seats of two-door cars. The important lesson to learn from this incident is to never make suggestions at management meetings unless you are prepared to implement them yourself, and from a manager's point of view, if somebody makes a suggestion at a meeting always propose that they are the ones who should implement it.

In contrast to this somewhat gritty experience, I must include a slightly strange one that occurred a few days later. I was standing by myself in the doorway of one of the steel cabins that enclosed the engine that drove one of the three big crude oil loading pumps. I had no shirt on and as I stood there I became aware of what must have been a small swirling vortex of breeze, which caressed my chest and shoulders. I stood for some time enjoying this pleasant and unusual experience. I had the strange feeling that this gentle massage was directed in some way and not just a random feature of the desert wind. I am not a believer in the supernatural but at the time I felt that, somehow, I may have been in the company of a desert djinn. A fanciful idea I think as I sit here writing about it forty years later but it seemed quite real at the time.

Soon after this I decided that two years at the Zueitina Oil Terminal was long enough and I persuaded one of the Libyan mechanics to apply for my job as a foreman. He had some influence and was promoted so one of the British foremen had to go; the process was called 'Libyanisation.' I volunteered for Libyanisation and was duly Libyanised. I left Libya never to return, with three months redundancy money, the largest wage packet I had ever had. I flew out from the desert airstrip at Zueitina on the 'Little Fokker' for the last time.

At this point, I was twenty-six years old. I owned a cottage in Lincolnshire, which I was renovating when home on field break. I had money in the bank and very quickly was recruited to work in the North Sea by Solar Gas Turbines who were part of International Harvester. The first thing they did was to send me to San Diego in California for six weeks training to be a 'Technical Representative' or 'tech rep'. Another name for a technician although some of the team called themselves 'Commissioning Engineers' in much the same way that plumbers call themselves 'Heating Engineers' and electricians call themselves 'Electrical Engineers.' If you haven't got a degree in engineering or you are not working at Engineer level then you are not an Engineer. That is unless you work shovelling coal on a steam engine, then I will allow that you are an 'engineer.'

When I was eighteen and I told the mother of a girlfriend that I was studying to be an 'Engineer'; she expressed her surprise as she didn't think that it required much training to shovel coal. This pretty much sums up the British attitude to technology, which is strange given that we started the industrial revolution and were responsible for so many important inventions. As my half German wife would say, 'It wouldn't happen in Germany.' Nor would it happen in France, Russia or the USA, but don't get me started.

Chapter 20   1976 WORKING OFFSHORE

Aged 27

'You're so detached you're separated'

The six week course in San Diego that Solar Gas Turbines sent me on was just fabulous as an experience of America in general, and California in particular. It seemed that every time I turned on the car radio they were playing 'Hotel California' by the Eagles. During the training course I lived in a 'Hotel California' with the other thirty delegates and after work I would go to the hotel bar for a beer before going out for the evening. Every night there was a band playing, they would stay for two weeks before moving on and being replaced by another act

I went out with an American girl while I was in San Diego; she felt that I was not very demonstrative.

'It's because as a Brit I am rather detached,' I said.

'Roger,' she said, 'you're so detached you're separated.'

One of the other delegates was an American of Mexican extraction called Salvador. He was a real gentleman. He lived locally, took me home to meet his family and showed me around generally. One morning as the class was about to start he remarked that I looked a little, pale.

'Yes Sal,' I said, 'last night I discovered Tequila.'

'No Roger,' said Sal with his slight Hispanic accent, 'last night Tequila discovered you.'

There is an urban myth that the grub, which lies curled up at the bottom of large bottles of Tequila, is there to impart flavour. In fact, it is there to prove that you are so drunk when you reach the bottom of the bottle that you will eat anything, even a grub. Thus the Mexican expression for a fellow who has a hangover is, 'He ate the grub last night.'

The trouble with the training course was that the training in gas turbine installation and maintenance was delivered exclusively in a classroom. We visited the factory once, and on no occasion did we work on, or touch, a gas turbine. The only way that I really learned anything was when I got back home and was sent out with another 'tech rep' to work on installations in Europe, N Africa and the N Sea. Eventually, my boss decided that I was competent to 'go it alone.' Off I went to deal with very large, dangerous and very expensive pieces of equipment, sometimes feigning a competence that I did not really feel.

On my first lone trip,, I travelled to a site in Tunisia. I flew into Carthage International Airport the night before, and after a twelve-hour drive across the desert in a Land Rover, I was confronted by a pair of large turbine engines, each driving a gas compressor. I had never seen a compressor before and they were connected to thirty-inch pipelines carrying gas at who knew what pressure and flow rate. I made my first examination in the company of various engineers and mechanics who obviously expected great things of me. I pressed the start button, the main valves opened; the machines started and ran up to speed over a minute or two. The Tunisian mechanics watched me as I looked wisely at the various gauges, tapped them a bit, as you do, and eventually pressed the stop button while nodding quietly to myself. The engines wound down to stop, again taking a minute or two, but one of the big main pipeline valves stayed open and a flare stack a few hundred metres away suddenly erupted with the most enormous roaring flame as all the gas flowing in the pipeline was diverted to it and began burning off. I was confronted with a scene from Hades. I looked at the flare stack, wishing that I were somewhere else. I had no idea what to do next. The mechanics looked at me. I looked at the flare stack again, said nothing and tried to look as if this was normal.

In the end one of the mechanics leaned forward, and with a small spanner tapped a micro switch, which was attached to a large valve just in front of us. The sticking switch activated the valve, which slowly closed, the flames subsided and silence reigned over the desert once again. I nodded to the mechanic as if this was just what I had expected and we all walked back to the tea hut where I began to quietly study the equipment manuals which were, of course, all in technical French, and therefore largely incomprehensible to me. I was much more careful about starting the equipment after that, but at least I knew that I had to tap the switch each time.

I stayed on this site for three weeks and was the only English speaker there. I had studied French at school for three years but could never pass an exam in the language. I could say all the right words, but not necessarily using the right tense. After my three-week 'total immersion course' both my French and my Arabic improved to the point that I could understand everything that was going on around me, although my spoken French is still at the Franglais level and all delivered in the present tense.

'Me no like it in desert, me go England after tomorrow.' My Arabic is much worse than this.

Chapter 21   1976 ECHO FISK

Aged 27

'Health and safety gone mad'

I was sent to Norway to do my first work offshore in the company of fellow employee Peter Schwegler, a German-speaking Swiss citizen. He was a very good technician but rather undiplomatic with customers. Whenever he was asked a question about the gas turbines that we were installing by oil company personnel, his answer would be an impatient, 'It's in ze manual.' I had played a nasty trick on him that morning in the hotel we stayed in before we travelled to the heliport in Stavanger to catch the helicopter out to Echo Fisk.

    I had woken up at about four am to get ready to catch the helicopter at about five am. As I was showering, there was a knock at the door of my hotel room and I grabbed a towel and opened it to find a very attractive Norwegian girl holding a bottle of beer and pretending to be a bit drunk. In fact, she was a 'lady of the night' touting for business. The clerk at the front desk had probably given her my room number what with me being young, male and on my own. I explained that I was delighted to meet her but was in a bit of a hurry and needed to catch a helicopter, then directed her to Peter's room, saying that he was a more likely customer.

    Later he muttered about his early morning visitor in the taxi on the way to the heliport. Her visit had offended his sense of propriety, he was very straight laced. Over the two weeks we spent off shore together, even when he was at his most annoying, I was able to remind myself that I had got the drop on him early on without him ever knowing.

The trip out to Echo Fisk was my first flight in a helicopter. I must say that it was very noisy, and flying without wings seemed unnatural somehow. Most of the passengers who were being dropped at various rigs were oil company employees and so they were given orange survival suits that were designed to keep them alive for some time if the helicopter ditched in the North Sea. They had reflective gold plated hoods, floatation, insulation and radio beacons to aid location. As contractors we were given nothing, presumably because we weren't worth saving. Fortunately, I had pair of ear defenders in my kit of turbine equipment so the noise didn't bother me unduly.

Echo Fisk is in the middle of the North Sea and in the Norwegian sector. We approached the complex of platforms that makes it up in the dark, and quite low and slowly. There was a flare boom at either end of the complex of about six platforms and the approach at low level with the heaving waters, the illumination from the flares reflecting on the water, the lights on the platform and the general strangeness of the situation, had a great effect on me. I could almost hear Wagner's 'Flight of the Valkyries,' playing in my ears. We landed on the helideck on the top of one of the platforms and I was nearly blown off by the wind as I got out of the helicopter.

We were given quarters on the platform and began work on the installation of the two large gas turbines that would be supplying some of the power required by the processes on board. I should explain at this point that the exploratory drilling of the North Sea had been performed during the nineteen sixties. The installation of the production platforms took place during the nineteen seventies, and this was what I was involved with. It was a bit like a Gold rush in that all sorts of people were getting involved, people who were not always qualified for the positions that they held. Even platform designs were sometimes questionable. The worst disaster in the North Sea was the 1988 fire on Piper Alpha platform, which, unbelievably, had decking made of wood in places.

The first day on Echo Fisk, I noticed that on one corner there was a cylindrical metal stump sticking up from the deck. It was about two metres high and about half that in diameter. There was a row of large gear teeth, which ran around the top. I asked one of the pipe fitters what it was. He told me that this was what was left of a crane. The gear teeth were part of the rotation system. The story was that the crane operator was only checked out for work on shore, not off shore, and had been lifting a large, very heavy equipment container from a supply vessel in rather a rough sea. The supply vessel rose on a huge wave, the crane operator took in the slack on the cable, the boat dropped into a trough and this applied the weight of the container on to the crane very suddenly. The whole crane was ripped from its mounting and, along with the container, went over the side of the platform narrowly missing the supply boat, and immediately sank the hundred metres or so to the bottom of the North Sea. I momentarily had a vivid impression of the horrified face of the operator as he lost control of his crane through his momentary lapse of judgement and then fell the several stories to his death as he hit the water. Divers recovered his body later

During the nineteen sixties, the American exploration companies had hired amateur divers from the UK, with no experience of deep diving and mixed gases. They were very well paid, but every year about ten percent of them were lost. Fortunately, safety is a much higher priority now that the North Sea installations are subject to inspection by the Health and Safety Executive. Previous to 1988, they had been subject to inspection by the Department of Energy and there may have been a slight conflict of interests. A question of giving the keys of the chicken shed to the fox. 'Health and safety,' - I can't get too much of it having seen what too little of it leads to.

That first night offshore as I lay in my bunk on the edge of sleep I was brought back to anxious consciousness by a loud crash. The platform shook. I found out later that one of the crane drivers had clumsily dropped a large container that he had just lifted off a supply boat onto the deck above our sleeping quarters. I was not yet used to the sights and sounds around me. As I lay, eyes wide open, wondering what would happen next a voice from the bunk above me muttered, 'One of the welders has dropped his wallet then.' I drifted off to sleep feeling reassured, as nobody else seemed to be worried. Always remember though that if you can keep you head while all around you are losing theirs then you probably do not understand the true seriousness of the situation.

There was always a big problem finding accommodation on oil rigs during the period of their construction. They would be designed to house the crew that would be needed to operate them, but during the construction phase there might be four times that many on board. Sometimes people would be flown back ashore if it was not too distant, but Echo Fisk is right in the middle of the North Sea, so another platform was towed out there to act as a hotel. This was the Alexander Kielland, a five-legged platform with accommodation, a mess hall, and a cinema on board. At the end of the working day, helicopters started to arrive at Echo Fisk to lift some of the workers over to the Alexander Kielland for the night. Two years after I gave up flying around the North Sea and went into a nice, safe teaching job, on a particularly cold night in March 1980, one of the legs suddenly broke off the Alexander Kielland and it immediately turned turtle and sank with the loss of 123 lives. Apparently most of the personnel were in the cinema watching a film at the time. I was quite shocked when I heard about it. There but for the grace of God etc. Apparently the designers thought that if the rig lost a leg it would remain stable on the remaining four, but, unfortunately, they had never tested their theory.

Chapter 22   1977 THE DESERT SONG

Aged 28

'This is a very sad song Monsieur.'

I landed at an oil field desert strip in Tunisia in 1977 with a fellow tech rep called Barry Smith. He was a fluent French speaker and had worked on this site before and was popular with the maintenance team, who were all Tunisians. He was a reasonably competent technician but when lack of knowledge required it he could sound convincing. This is a useful talent when you are constantly being presented with equipment that you have never seen before, nor been briefed about, in places where you can't even speak the language or read the manuals. Barry was a Francophile, who liked a drink and a laugh. His sense of humour, however, could, on occasion, be rather dangerous. Three Tunisian technicians who knew Barry had come to the airstrip, in a Land Rover, to collect us and drive us back to the base.

'Bonjour, mes braves, I have come to make love to all your women in order to improve the Tunisian race,' said Barry, in perfect French except that he didn't say, 'Make love.'

Unaccountably, the technicians all laughed and clapped him on the back and said, 'Oh Monsieur Barry. Ha, ha, ha.'

I am glad that they found his racial insults funny because if they hadn't we might have been found buried under a sand dune three weeks later, with our throats cut, and nobody the wiser back in Blighty.

Some people can say anything and get a laugh. I, on the other hand, cannot. An Algerian mechanic once asked at coffee time, which religion I practiced.

'Oh,' I said airily, 'Buddhism.' I was trying to divert him.

'But Monsieur Roger, the Buddhists they don't believe in Allah,' he replied. I had forgotten that Muslims are often quite knowledgeable about other religions; it is part of their religious education. There was a wary pause, and I could sense the other mechanics mentally contemplating the Koranic instruction concerning unbelievers and metaphorically running their thumbs along the blades of their imaginary curly knives.

'The Book or the Sword,' a Palestinian friend had once told me when we were working together in Libya. He was explaining the policy of Saladin when converting the peoples that he had conquered to Islam. I decided that in future, when asked, I would profess membership of the Church of England. It's so much simpler and safer.

Most Muslims, accept Christianity and Judaism to some extent as, like Islam, they rely on the Old Testament for their basis, and therefore, are collectively known as the 'Religions of the Book.' Not believing in anything is not to be advertised. Don't be an infidel is my advice.

Barry and I were scheduled to work on this site for the usual three weeks. On our first evening, which was a Sunday, our meal consisted of horrible tasting black sausages of unidentifiable origin. Neither I nor Barry, who considered himself a gourmet, could eat them. On the Monday, we were served stewed mutton and vegetables for lunch and then the same for dinner. On the Tuesday, we were once again served stewed mutton and vegetables for lunch and dinner. On the Wednesday, the same, and indeed for the rest of the week there was no variation until Sunday came around, and then we were served delicious black sausages with an interesting flavour which made a welcome change.

Tunisia was the only North African country where we were given a bottle of beer with our evening meal. Everybody had a bottle of beer, Muslims, Christians, and even infidels. After a couple of weeks, Barry was called from our head office in London and told to go to another site. I was due to go home in one more week but the site superintendent wanted me to stay and finish the job I was working on rather than have to wait for another tech rep, who might not appear for some time, and would not be familiar with what I had been doing.

As part of the process of talking me into staying, they supplied Barry and me with some extra bottles of their surprisingly strong beer after dinner in the canteen that evening. At some point during the discussions I felt that it was incumbent upon me to sing a song to entertain the twenty or so technicians and mechanics, who were still finishing their meals and who, it must be said, had offered me no encouragement in this venture. However, I decided to sing my signature song 'Your baby has gone down the plughole,' which, I felt, would bring some humour to the proceedings.

As I sang about the baby being so thin that it was, 'Only a skellington covered with skin,' and how, as the mother turned away to get the soap, the baby slid down the plug hole, never to be seen again, Barry translated the song line by line while I paused in my singing to let him do so.

At the end of my performance, I was puzzled at the quiet and serious faces around me until the superintendent broke the silence by clearing his throat and saying, somewhat formally, 'That was a very sad song, Monsieur.' I realised that the humour had somehow, been lost in translation. Either that or North

A Horse in the Morning

Africans, for some reason, do not find the idea of starving babies funny.

Eventually, I finished the work on the engines, left the site and flew to Amsterdam Schiphol airport on my way to the next job. I was in a hurry as I checked in for my next flight, and was pleased with my coolness under pressure. I placed my clamshell briefcase on the counter, opened it, handed over my tickets and passport, and received my boarding card. The rather beautiful, blonde, Dutch girl that I was dealing with was impressed with all the stamps in my passport; it was obvious to her that I was an experienced traveller, she smiled attractively as I grabbed my briefcase, which I had forgotten to fully close and lock. I took hold of the handle and with a last wry smile at her hurried away from her desk trailing money, documents, small tools and a bottle of whiskey which smashed on the tiled floor. Seldom have I felt so deflated. Pride comes before a fall.

If ever you take a taxi from Schiphol Airport, the taxi driver will inevitably tell you that the airport is five metres below sea level. Every time. If you tell them that you already know this, they get all huffy, so show an interest and say,

'Really?' And try to sound convincing. This is just a traveler's tip.

The words to the song 'Your baby has gone down the plug hole,' are in the Appendices.

Chapter 23   1977 ABERDEEN AIRPORT

Aged 28

'You just fly the helicopter mate and leave the clever stuff to me!'

I had been sent to work on the new four-hundred-acre oil terminal on the island of Flotta in the Orkney Islands just North of Scotland. My company, International Harvester, had eight gas turbines on the site and I was one of the team of tech reps who were rotated on a continuous basis to connect them up, and get them running. Our company had engines all over Europe, the North Sea and North Africa, and because of all the construction and installation work in the North Sea, there were not enough tech reps to look after them all. Customers (usually oil companies) were not always happy about the service they received, but it is difficult to find people who are competent and familiar with the equipment, or alternatively, to train them.

I had been posted up to Flotta and pretty much left to work for the summer with odd weekends home to my bachelor cottage in Lincolnshire. I was quite happy on Flotta, I even had a girlfriend who worked on the site, and lived in a caravan nearby. There were hundreds of men working there, living in prefabricated barracks, one small room to each man. There were about six women working there in various capacities, but they were not allowed to live on the site. American oils companies had a rather puritanical attitude.

As a matter of interest, the sea to the North of Flotta is called Scapa Flow and at the end of the First World War, the German fleet was interned there awaiting surrender to the allies when peace negotiations were complete. In the event, after nine months of waiting and under the orders of Admiral von Reuter, the officer in command, the fleet was scuttled to prevent them falling into British hands, and there they lie at the bottom of the sea to this day. When anybody local complained of an oil spill from the terminal on Flotta the oil companies blamed the leaking fuel tanks of the German fleet.

One morning, I was told that I was needed on the Piper Alpha platform in the North Sea. It was owned by Occidental Petroleum, and this was the company that I was working for on Flotta so there was no conflict of interest. The problem on Piper Alpha was that the gas turbine which ran the emergency generator on the platform would not start, so in theory the platform must be shut down and abandoned because if there was a fire, the sea water fire pumps would not run. Of course, everybody scoffed at the idea that there would be a fire on Piper Alpha but the company had to take their insurance policy seriously. On the other hand the platform was producing millions of pounds worth of oil every day and Occidental was not going to stop production without very good reason. They needed me out there to start their engine and thus validate their insurance policy and money was no object. Suddenly, and for the only time in my life, I was in a key position and, briefly, an important player. Yes, I was a 'contender!'

I felt pretty important as I climbed aboard the small plane, which Oxy hired for me. It was not a lot bigger that the Piper Cherokee that I had learned to fly about ten years before at Elstree airfield. I wondered if the pilot would let me have a go at the controls if I told him my Graham Hill story and mentioned that I had done my first solo flight. Well, as there were two other passengers, and one of them was the deputy terminal superintendent, I didn't even ask. I politely opened the door for the other passengers and helped them to get aboard and thus, being the last to board, snaffled the right-hand front seat for myself while they sat in the back. I enjoyed the flight to Aberdeen, which was at lower level than usual and over some spectacular Scottish scenery. I even found out a bit about air navigation. It's much easier than you think.

At Aberdeen airport heliport arrivals desk, they didn't know anything about flying me out to Piper Alpha of course. The manager slowly and carefully explained to me that the airport was about to close, and that it would cost tens of thousands of pounds to keep it open just to fly one rather unimpressive looking technician out in a helicopter all by himself. The cost of the helicopter hire would also be prohibitive. Perhaps I would like to come back tomorrow and see about a seat on one of the regular flights to Piper Alpha?

I asked them to call their contact at Occidental, which was one of their most important customers. Eventually, the guy behind the desk became worried enough by my insistence that they complied. The Occidental rep verified my story and suddenly everything changed. Would I like to have a seat? Would I like a cup of coffee? What colour helicopter would I like to fly in? Actually, I made the last one up. Eventually, a dashing looking pilot appeared at the door of the ready room wearing a uniform, headphones and other heroic looking technical accoutrements. I was the only occupant of the room, wearing jeans, a parka and accompanied by the two cases of tools and instruments that I needed to perform my duties. He looked at me with a puzzled expression, shook his head and left. He returned a few minutes later to ask me sarcastically where the 'big engineer' was and what was so important about me that I merited my own transport out to Piper

Alpha on an emergency basis late at night, keeping the airport open and generally inconveniencing people? What I should have said was, 'You just fly the helicopter mate, and leave the clever stuff to me.'

A less truthful author would lie, but I have to report that unfortunately I could not think of a witty riposte at the time and just muttered something about emergency generators. He accompanied me to a larger helicopter, I climbed into the darkened passenger compartment, which had about two dozen empty seats in it, and off we went. He wouldn't let me sit up front with him. I did have a chat with him en route using the headphones that I had been given. I explained the situation on Piper Alpha to him. I expect that he was glad of the overtime really.

As we flew over the North Sea, in the noise and darkness, in separate parts of the helicopter, and listening to each other's disembodied voices in our headphones, he told me that he would love to have a job like mine, being flown all over the world to exciting places, working on interesting equipment, and meeting unusual people. He said that he felt like a bus driver some times.

Really, I thought. I'd always wanted to be a pilot. But I wasn't going to tell him that, not after he'd pissed me off in the ready room. I managed to give the impression that it was all in a day's work for me, which, at that time, I suppose that it was.

We landed on the platform and I am happy to say that I had the engine running within the hour because, although I may not always give that impression in these writings, I was quite good at my job and knew a thing or two about big engines.

Having got their emergency generator working, Occidental suddenly found that they did not have any empty seats available on helicopters leaving their platform for the foreseeable future. This was an example of a well-known syndrome in the emotional life of site and platform superintendents called 'kidnapping the manufacturer's representative.' It was usually caused by lack of confidence that the equipment in question would not break down again. I had seen it all before and was quite happy to have a few days rest while my boss attempted to make the oil company give me back. My charge-out rate was astronomical, but this was of no concern to an oil company, which was making millions of dollars a day. There was the usual problem finding accommodation for me. My visit was not planned, so I was given the operating table in the sickbay, surrounded by lockers and medical equipment. Not for the first time I woke up next morning to find that I was apparently in hospital having presumably suffered some horrifying accident. It took a moment to work out where I was and also a certain amount of feeling myself all over to see if all my limbs and appendages were still intact. I always hated waking up in the sick bay.

It is worth noting that in 1988, ten years after my visit, there was a terrible explosion on Piper Alpha caused by poor attention to safety procedures. The resulting enormous oil and gas fire was the worst accident that had happened in the North Sea. One hundred and sixty-seven men lost their lives and the overall financial loss was £1.7 billion. The platform was at a junction in the pipelines that took oil and gas from various other fields. The platform superintendents in the other fields would not shut down the flow of product to Piper Alpha without direct orders from their head offices in the USA. They continued to feed the fire that they could clearly see burning over the horizon. The problem is that loss of production equates to loss of enormous amounts of money, and heads will roll if the wrong decision is made. So they waited for somebody else, thousands of miles away, to make the decision, while good men died.

Chapter 24   1978 THE GIRL ON THE UNDERGROUND PLATFORM

Aged 27

There was only one gas platform off the southern tip of Ireland in the late seventies because that was the only field that had been discovered. My company had two turbines on board driving electrical generators. I was sent out to continue the installation that was partially completed and was given the usual gang of fitters and electricians to connect up all the instrumentation and align the engines to the generators. One of the electricians was working on a bank of starting batteries. These batteries performed the same function as the battery in your car except they were used to start a gas turbine and there were a lot of them all connected together. The electrician put one end of a spanner on a battery terminal, and as he tightened it, the other end of the spanner touched the metal side of the battery box resulting in the whole bank of batteries attempting to discharge through his spanner. There was an impressive flash, and two of the batteries exploded.

Nobody likes flashes and bangs when they are not expecting them, especially electricians and especially on gas platforms. We looked over at the battery box and there was the electrician standing stock still, shocked, presumably wondering whether he was dead or not. It would have been quite funny but for the fact that he was covered in battery acid, and as the platform was not fully serviceable we had no water supply with which to hose him down. His foreman did not seem a bit concerned, so I and the trainee tech rep that was with me, grabbed him by the arms and rushed him down many flights of steps and over the gangplank to our support barge to hose him down. It turned out that the batteries were of the alkaline type, not acid, and apparently the alkali is less corrosive than acid, so he was not badly burned. I was not impressed by the lack of concern shown by the electrician's supervisor, but this was not unusual.

To give an example of the cavalier attitude of the construction bosses on that project, when I had first arrived by helicopter on the support barge, I found that to get across to the gas platform, a long ladder had been laid flat from the handrail of the barge to the lower access stage of the gas platform, a plank was laid on top of the ladder so that personnel could walk over it, there was no hand rail. As the gas platform was anchored to the seabed and the barge was not, the ladder was going up and down with the motion of the waves at one end while the other was stationary. The two were separated by about fifteen metres. When I suggested to the superintendent that this was very dangerous, he pointed to a rope with floats, which was in the water about two storeys below us and assured me that when somebody had fallen in the week before, they had got him out of the water within a few minutes.

I explained that if I fell in with the two cases of equipment that I was carrying, then the equipment would be lost and I could not do my job. I would have to wait days or weeks for replacement kit to be flown out from our head office in San Diego, and this was not going to get his turbines running was it? He realised that the equipment at least was valuable if not the contractor, and with a heavy sigh he called up the crane driver on his radio to lift me across in a personnel basket. This sounds like a nice ride at a park. It was not. The deck of the gas platform was a long way above the sea and the crane operator lifted me all the way from sea level to the top helideck at speed, while I clung to the outside of the personnel basket. I am sure that you have seen this on the television. Frankly, the only way that I could get through the experience was to keep my eyes shut for most of the ride. I'm sure that one gets used to it in the end - the nonchalant oil-men on the TV didn't seem to worry. Even though I **am all right** with normal heights, this was 'pushing the envelope' and, in future, I walked the plank between the barge and the platform. The supervisor was kind enough not to mention it, but he knew that he had won.

Because there was no accommodation available on the barge, at the end of the working day, we were helicoptered back to Cork where we stayed in a hotel. Luckily, we were close enough to the shore to do this; the trip took about half an hour. In those days, there were not a lot of helicopters flying around the Irish Republic and when we landed at Cork airport the observation balcony **was** full of people leaning over the railing to get a look at the 'Oil Men.' Being the callow youth that I was, I swaggered across the tarmac wearing my bright yellow hard hat, which made me even more conspicuous. Seeing this, one of the reps that I was working with burst my bubble by snatching my hard hat from my head and booting it down the taxiway so that I was forced to ignominiously scamper after it under the amused gaze of seemingly hundreds of Irish people all laughing and pointing from the observation deck. I stopped showing off after that.

The company's head office **was** in Knightsbridge, London, opposite the Horse Guards Barracks. Every few weeks, I would appear in the offices to submit my expenses and receive briefings and assignments. I was friendly, in the nicest possible way, with the girls who did the admin work and on my last day there several of them took me out to the newly opened 'Hard Rock Cafe' for a farewell beer and a burger. At the end of the meal we said **goodbye** and I set off for home on the Underground. As I was waiting on the platform at one of the stations, I noticed a girl who was standing rather close to the edge looking tearful and distressed. She was looking into the tunnel and talking to herself, quite honestly I thought that she was going to jump in front of the next train. I exchanged concerned looks with a couple of other people standing on the platform and, in the end, as the train came into the station, and feeling rather hesitant, I walked up behind the girl, put my hands on her shoulders and moved her back while saying something reassuring. Considering the way that I had invaded her personal space she was remarkably unresponsive at first but, in the end, she shrugged me off, angrily leaving the platform muttering without a backward glance.

I have often wondered what that was about and had the strange feeling that I was supposed to be there to intervene at that moment. It sounds fanciful, but at the time I felt that it was possible that my whole life had been leading to that point and that, from now on, Fate had no further interest in me. This was my second slightly metaphysical experience, the first one being the djinn in the Libyan desert breeze a couple of years before.

Soon after this, I left the oilfields and went to Nottingham University for a year to train to be a teacher. I'd had enough of this life of living on platforms or trailers in the desert, staying in hotels, flying around in helicopters and generally living on my wits. I'd bought a house, had money in the bank and met the girl of my dreams. I was twenty-nine and wanted to settle down and lead a more regular life.

One of the things that surprised me at

Nottingham University was the immaturity of the fellow graduates who were on the course with me. I'd always had a slight chip on my shoulder because I got my degree at a Polytechnic rather than at a 'proper' university, and I expected that these people would be a slightly superior breed to me. I was only a few years older than the others on the course and some of them were very clever and articulate, but they hadn't done anything. In a strange sort of way, they seemed to be children while I felt quite adult. Some of them even found it difficult to get up and to be on time for lectures. I wondered how they would handle the normal discipline of a full time job. I am sure that the University of Life knocked them into shape quite quickly.

PART THREE MANHOOD

And responsibility

Chapter 25   1980 ALTERNATIVE SOLUTIONS

Aged 31

'So, the dog ate it I suppose?'

The parents of my friend Alan, who had participated in the disappearance of my bubble car at Barnet College in 1967, owned a caravan at Mundesley in Norfolk. Adam and I had holidayed there when we were teenagers and financed the trips by fruit and bean picking on the nearby farms. One of the local girls, Valerie, who for some reason I remember wearing a pink bikini at the time, was the fifteen-year-old version of the woman that I would later marry. I was eighteen at that time.

In the latter part of my work in the North Sea I had met Valerie once more at Adam and his wife's house. I courted her for about a year and a half, mainly while I was studying for my teaching qualification, and we were married in 1979 at Mundesley Church. I bought a house that needed serious work done to it and we settled down to our first five years of marriage. More of this later.

I took up my first teaching post at the age of thirty, working as a Technology teacher at Framingham Earl High School, a comprehensive school in Norfolk just south of Norwich. I was very lucky to start my teaching career at such a pleasant school working under the excellent headmaster of the time, Mr Ernest Forbes.

While on playground duty one morning I noticed a boy who was engrossed with a strange **multi-coloured** object which he was manipulating with both hands as he walked around the playground. I suspected that this might be one of the 'Rubik's Cubes' that I had heard about but had never seen, as they were still very new at that time. I went over and asked him if I could have a look at it and was intrigued by the way that the lesser cubes could be moved independently around the main body. I asked him if I could take it into the staffroom to show to some of the other teachers at lunchtime and he agreed.

A small group of us sat down at a circular coffee table, a scientist, an artist and an engineer. I placed the Cube in the centre of the table and we each took a turn with it but could not come anywhere near to solving it. Obviously, I wanted I give it back with all six sides covered by squares of the same colour, as the solution required.

The scientist tried to solve the Cube conventionally. I, the **technologist**, daringly suggested that we take it apart and reassemble it in the correct order. The art teacher, however, lackadaisically suggested that all we had to do was to peel all the stickers off and carefully stick them back in the required places. Later on in my career when I taught engineering design I used to use this as an example of both lateral thinking and brainstorming. All of the solutions would have worked, but the Art teacher's solution was the one most easily achieved while expending the least effort.

In the end, I gave the Cube back unsolved.

The art teacher was a potter originally and still practiced his art in his workshop at home. With the permission of the science department, he had made the mistake of borrowing a chemical balance from the school to help accurately measure the constituents of the glazes that he used in his home kiln. He rented out a couple of bedrooms in his house to some rather shady characters because, since his divorce, he could not afford the mortgage. The police busted the premises and found rather a lot of illegal substances there and they used the possession of the chemical balance as evidence of drug dealing and he was duly arrested. The science teacher appeared in court as a character witness and explained the presence of the chemical balance but to no avail. The art teacher served a year in prison and was never allowed in a classroom again. This was a great shame because he was an imaginative teacher and very popular with the pupils.

After I had been teaching for a couple of years, I had learned the need to start as you mean to go on when it comes to getting pupils to hand work in on time. I explained to a new group that I was going to set some homework and would expect it to be handed in next lesson or trouble would ensue. A week later, all the pupils handed in the homework except one boy who promised to hand it in the next week. Apparently, he had been , 'Rubbing lard on the cat's boil,' 'His mother was having twins,' and 'His father was coming out of prison' or something. Anyway, he pleaded 'family business' so I gave him another week. When the work still didn't appear, I explained to him that the gap in my mark book was not going to fill itself, and that if the homework didn't appear next week then he could expect to be in detention. The next week the conversation went something like this:

'Well, George, have you done the homework that I gave you?'

'Yes, sir.'

I was surprised but I did not show it, being not inexperienced at this sort of negotiation.

'Have you got it with you then?'

'No, sir.'

Just as I had expected.

'So, the dog ate it I suppose?'

'No sir, I did the homework last night and put it

in the inside pocket of my jacket so as not to forget it. I set off for school on my bike this morning but as I rode along I heard a strange humming sound and looking up, I found that a huge metal disc was hovering above me and keeping pace with my bike. Suddenly there was a high-pitched whirring sound and two doors in the underneath slid back, a beam of green light like a laser beam shone down straight into my pocket and then went back into the disc carrying my homework. The whirring came again, the doors slid back into place, the humming got louder and suddenly the disc flew away over the horizon faster than an aeroplane.'

I gave him a B+. In my opinion, and speaking with a special interest, I feel that storytellers should be treasured.

After a couple of years of teaching at secondary level I realised that not only did I have more to offer in further and higher education with my engineering experience, but also the job was much more interesting and discipline easier. I specialised in teaching computer-aided design and eventually rapid prototyping.

When I first started teaching at Lowestoft College of Further and Higher Education, my staff room was inhabited by some colourful characters. Two of the senior lecturers were David Smoyles and Jim Baker. The first was a man who, in the nicest possible way, was always on the lookout for a dodge or advantage; he was, as they say in Suffolk, 'all about.' The other was a quiet fellow who smoked a pipe, stared into the distance and just seemed generally quite satisfied with his lot; he was not an excitable man. One day Keith said to Jim,

'Lend us your car mate.'

Jim, who was enjoying his pipe at the time, dug into his jacket pocket, pulled out his keys, handed them to Keith and carried on smoking and thinking. He didn't ask what Keith wanted the car for. What I didn't know at the time was that both men owned Ford Cortinas of the same model and colour, but in very different states of repair. Jim's car was in tip top working order while David's was rather down at heel with worn tyres, rusted bodywork and an oil leak.

Keith went out to the car park and taking out his **screwdriver**, swapped the number plates of the cars over and drove Jim's car to an MoT testing station, where it passed the yearly test with flying colours. Very pleased with himself he drove back to the staff car park, swapped the number plates back and put the new MoT test certificate in the glove compartment of his wrecked old car. Returning to the staffroom he gave Jim his keys back, sat down and started marking some assignments humming quietly. Jim carried on puffing on his pipe and staring into the distance.

Don't try this yourself, the mechanics at the MoT testing stations check the chassis numbers these days.

Chapter 26   1982 DOWSING

Aged 33

'The younger ones think that I'm bonkers.'

I mentioned before that I am not a believer in the supernatural, but the third slightly strange thing that I observed concerned the activities of a certain official from the local water company.

Using the funds I saved from my four years of working in the desert and offshore, I had bought a house for me and my wife to live in. This was before we had children. We were 'dinkies' that is 'double income no kids.' The house was in a nice little Norfolk village called Wickhampton. We made good friends there and had a very happy time renovating and extending our big old house over several years while I worked as a teacher and she worked as a pharmacist.

One day, I realised that I had no idea where the outside stop tap for the water supply was. I knew where the one inside was, under the kitchen sink as you would expect, but the outside one was a bit of a mystery. I looked on the pavement outside our house but to no avail, so in the end I rang the water company.

It was the summer holidays for teachers and pupils so, although my wife was at work, I was at home renovating when, some days after my phone call, a man came around in a van to find my stop tap. I gave him the obligatory cup of tea, we chatted about the well at the front of the house, in which he had a professional interest. He was interested in all things 'watery,' as he put it.

He began his search, he looked and looked but

he could not find that stop tap. After about a quarter of an hour he went back to his van and brought out a pair of stiff wires bent at right angles into 'L' shapes. The wire was probably from a wire coat hanger, it was about that thick. Loosely holding the short side of a wire in each hand he moved his wrists until both wires were pointing forwards so that they were horizontal and parallel to each other. He looked over at me and said, 'The younger ones think that I'm bonkers when I do this, but it works.'

He slowly walked along the footpath next to our hedge. A little way from my front gate the wires began to move and eventually they crossed. He noted where this was and continued walking, the wires uncrossed and returned to their former state, parallel to each other. He made a chalk mark on the ground, and then went into our garden and did the same thing with a similar result on the other side of the hedge. He sighted a line between the two points that he had found, and with a little bit of effort and a shovel, soon found the stop tap. Job done and with my gratitude, he drove off.

Being the sceptic that I am, I thought, he knew where that stop tap was. He saw it while he was searching and did that little pantomime for my benefit. So I went into the house, found a coat hanger, went into my workshop and made myself a pair of 'dowsing rods,' for that is what they were.

I tried a bit of 'dowsing' myself but as I knew where the pipe was I really couldn't call it a scientific test, and it was at this point that my wife came home from work. Some weeks earlier I had visited her at the pharmacy at the rear of the shop in Norwich where she was employed, and on seeing her and her two dispensers counting tablets and mixing potions had remarked, somewhat tactlessly, that three hundred years ago, they would probably all have been burned at the stake. I laughed, nobody else did, and I had to buy cream cakes at coffee time to repair the damage

Back in the present and without explaining, I put the dowsing rods in her hands, told her how to hold them and asked her to walk along the footpath outside the house to see what would happen. The rods crossed as she walked over the place that I knew the water pipe was buried.

Well, I thought, just a fluke. She hadn't noticed what had happened and carried on walking. As she came level with the meter box set in the outside wall of our house, the rods crossed again as they passed over the underground mains cable where it was buried under the footpath. Again, she didn't seem to notice, and I had certainly never discussed underground cables with her. She turned around as she reached our neighbours fence.

'Can I stop now?' she asked.

'Yes, best that you stop now,' I said, and felt a certain level of vindication.

The five years that we lived in and renovated this house together were a very happy time in my life. We were both young, in love, without financial pressures or the responsibility of children. We had some memorable holidays and were lucky enough to have good friends and neighbours, some of whom I am still in touch with. Parenthood certainly has its compensations, but 'Dinkyhood 'was very good.

Chapter 27 1984 A MEMORABLE CHARACTER

Aged 35

'I expect that the irony will escape him.'

Edward Wilson, described in the Tribune as 'the thinking person's John Le Carre,' has published five books. 'A River in May' was the author's semi-autobiographical first novel set in the Vietnam War during which he served as a Lieutenant in the US Special Forces. He has, so far, published a quartet of Cold War spy novels.

I first met Ted in 1985 while he was still teaching English at Lowestoft College of Further Education. At the time, I was a relative newcomer to the staff room and on the day in question a group of mainly female lecturers were sitting around a large circular table discussing playground bullying. Every one of the staff members seemed to have a tale to tell about having been bullied at school or their child had been bullied, or their goldfish had been bullied by a larger fish. Nobody admitted to have done any bullying themselves. Personally, I remember being involved on both sides of that particular coin during my school days but, rather like divorcees, the party telling the story is always blameless. Over at a corner table, a newspaper was rustled impatiently to the sound of a muttered expletive.

'Yes that's the trouble with children who get bullied,' said a voice from behind the staff room copy of the Times Educational Supplement. 'They all have something wrong with them, a gammy leg or a hole in the heart or they suck up to the teachers.'

An uncomfortable silence ensued, there was a further impatient rustle of the paper and as it was time to get back to the 'chalk face,' we all left.

Ted's active service in Vietnam had left him with a somewhat Darwinian view of personal relationships. His obvious 'liberal' leanings endeared him to me, however, and we struck up a lasting friendship, which continued after his early retirement from teaching and the beginnings of his new writing career. Teaching was not to be the last refuge of this particular scoundrel.

Occasionally, we would go sea fishing from his sailing cruiser moored in the estuary at Orford. This was Ted's 'weekend cottage' where he loitered aboard in solitary splendour or sometimes accompanied by his partner Celia on Saturdays and Sundays, swimming in the cold, cloudy waters, drinking wine in the evenings and, sometimes, catching a fishy dinner. Famously, on one occasion, he accidentally caught a large lobster on a hook and line. I would have liked to have witnessed the meeting on the deck between these two equally crustaceous individuals.

On our fishing days, Ted was always optimistic about the state of the tide and the appetites of the fish.

'The tide is on the turn, they'll start to bite at any minute.'

Thirty bite-free minutes would go by and he would have another theory.

'Low water will bring them to the bait.'

After several unsuccessful expeditions, where neither of us got a bite let alone caught a fish, Ted looked at me thoughtfully one afternoon and said, 'We never catch anything when you're on board.'

I knew that in his mind it was my fault that we would once again be returning ashore, dishonoured by our deficiencies in the hunter-gatherer department. We tried fishing from kayaks, dinghies and even the shore, but only on one occasion did we have any significant luck, and that was when somebody else piloted the boat and showed us where to fish. Unreasonably, we felt, he insisted on taking a third of our catch!

Ted went through a phase of trying to irritate the CIA by phoning me and starting the conversation with the words, 'Bomb, President, Al Qaeda.'

I could almost hear the disk drives at Langley whirling up to speed and the clicks on the telephone line as the silent listener's attentions were directed our way. I found myself making vain protestations of my innocence in an attempt to placate them, as I pictured two men in black suits with American accents knocking on my door at two o'clock the next morning. Ted had given up his American citizenship years before due to his disagreements with US foreign policy. He was a bit of a Leftie.

After the publication of his Vietnam War novel, 'A River in May' I saw him in a totally different light.

'Did all of those things happen to you?' I asked. Many of the 'things' in the book had been quite horrifying.

'Not all of them happened to me, some of them happened to people I knew.'

I found out later that the citation associated with one of his medals described him leading his platoon through 'withering automatic fire,' with fifteen of his men evacuated as casualties. It made my adventures in the 'Oil Patch' seem rather tame.

Ted could be sensitive about certain things, however. One day, when I was visiting him and we were having a cup of tea, two 'good old Suffolk boys' delivered his winter supply of coal. He remarked after they had left, 'Now they are going to think that I'm a homosexual.' I asked him why? 'Well, two men, alone, drinking tea. It's obvious.'

I live in a rural location and one day I found a

dead Fallow deer, recent road kill but still warm, near my house. I rang Ted, feeling that his training with Special Forces would have equipped him to deal with this situation.

'Take it home,' he said, 'I'll be straight round.'

My wife and I struggled to load the deer into the back of my car. With some difficulty Ted and I hung it up from a rafter in my garage and, somewhat inexpertly, we butchered it. I have a lasting memory of Ted on his knees, engaged in the grisly business, hands red. He turned around, smiled thinly, as he looked up at me through his frameless glasses.

'This is the best thing we have ever done together,' he said. I felt a slight sense of unease as I looked at the knife in his hand.

'Yes,' I said faintly, 'I suppose it is.'

On another occasion, he rang me because he had hurt his wrist, and wanted my advice. My son is a doctor and therefore, obviously, I have telepathic access to all his knowledge.

'Have it X-rayed,' I suggested.

'No, I don't want to get medicalised,' he spat.

This was a word with which I was unfamiliar at the time.

'It will heal up on its own eventually,' said the steely-eyed paratrooper.

'Healing up on its own' involved continuous pain, swelling and spectacularly multicoloured bruising. When he was eventually forced to visit the hospital he was criticised by the saw-bones who treated his complicated fracture for 'late presentation'. He has not played tennis since.

Soon after his visit to the hospital we met in the pedestrian precinct in Halesworth, our local market town. It was a cold winter's day, snow and ice covered the ground. He proudly showed his plaster cast, and we set off together seeking refreshment. I went to help him over a slippery patch at the entrance to the Angel Hotel. Ted angrily pushed my hand away, nearly falling over in the process.

'I'm not going in there holding hands,' he said. 'What will people think?'

In 2007, Ted won the Independent on Sunday 'Skills Every Man Should Have' competition by supplying, as they characterised it 'a refreshingly un-PC top 20'. Amongst which were:

Challenge a liar to a duel.

Hide a fugitive Jesuit in a priest hole.

Treat prisoners with dignity

Overthrow global capitalism.

Joke with the executioner as you place your head on the block.

As Ted's oeuvre grew, I was pleased to see him gain serious success. The Chinese have a saying that 'there is nothing so satisfying as to see a good friend fall off a roof,' but my feelings for Ted's new career were always entirely encouraging in those early days. Naively, I made the mistake of asking him whether or not he had used me as a template for any of his fictional characters.

'Absolutely not,' he assured me, implying that I was not nearly interesting enough.

'Anyway,' he said, 'you look like a pilot.' I have never been sure what he meant by that.

He became surprisingly interested in the fact that although I call myself by my second name 'Roger,' my first name is 'Gerald'; and in his fourth Cold War book 'The Whitehall Mandarin' he introduced a minor character, a field officer whose real name was 'Gerald' but who used the code name 'Roger.' I was flattered by this inclusion and read on with mounting interest, curious as to the activities of this exciting alter ego. It transpired that when the Red Army engaged in military exercises on the German plains in the 1960's the soldiers were not issued with toilet paper, and so they used whatever paper they could find, including maps, pages from equipment manuals and code books. All were potentially valuable sources of information to Western Intelligence and so after the exercise they were secretly collected by Gerald's local agents, bagged up and handed over to him for processing and information extraction.'

I haven't seen much of Edward Wilson recently. I believe that he is currently engaged in the production of a fifth espionage novel in which, much to the author's amusement, 'Gerald's' activities are extended, but in much the same mode. If and when it is published I have every intention of hanging it on a nail in my 'smallest room' and reading a few pages a day.

The phrase 'flush fiction' comes to mind but, as Ted is an American, I expect that the irony will escape him.

Chapter 28   1985 THE CHILD IS FATHER TO THE MAN

Aged 36

Having recently been introduced to my first grandson, and as the process of my 'Grandaddification' begins, I think about my time as the father of my two small boys Tom and Harry, twenty-five and more years ago. I can remember some of the priceless things that they said and did. The boys were five and three years old when I became what my American aunt called a 'Disneyland Dad.' My wife and I were divorced and the boys went to live with her and her new partner. I retained the marital home and the boys and I spent a lot of quality time together at weekends and on holidays. It was probably because of my wish to spend time with them that I did not get married again until about twenty years later. I certainly did not want to start a new family; I preferred to stick with the one I had.

At about the age of four, my first son was always anxious to tell me about things that he had discovered that day when I arrived home from work. He would start the conversation with the phrase, 'And did you know, Dad?' and continue with things like, 'Spiders have eight legs,' or 'blue and yellow make green.'

One day I came home and he said, 'And did you know, Dad, that you don't have to take two bottles into the shower because you can Wash and Go?' At this time, he thought that adverts on the TV were public information films.

Soon after this, we went on holiday to Scotland with several other family members including his four-year-old cousin Mary whose birthday we celebrated. One of Mary's presents was a nurse's uniform. As I sat reading in the sunshine in the garden of our rented house one morning a little voice said, 'Look at me, Dad.'

I looked up and there was Tom wearing Mary's nurse's outfit including the dress and cap.

'You look great,' I said as I lifted my camera and took the photograph, which would haunt his teenage years.

When Tom was about five and Harry was about three, the two boys were having a friendly wrestle on the floor when Harry coughed full in Tom's face. He was disgusted and said, 'Ergh, now I've got your germs.'

Harry thought about this for a moment, oblivious to the hygiene implications and thinking that Tom had taken something of his, he growled, 'Give me back my germs.'

At Tom's direction, he had to lie on his back with his mouth wide open while Tom coughed them back into him. This was perfectly logical of course but not very sanitary. Surprisingly, Tom was to become a doctor some years later after this somewhat dubious beginning in the field microbiology.

When Tom was seven and Harry was five I took them to see Father Christmas at his grotto in Selfridges in London. We asked a policeman on Oxford Street if he knew where the old chap could be found. He was most helpful and directed us to the department store in question. We didn't have to queue for very long as there had been a bomb scare. There were actually several Santa's, carefully screened off from little eyes and, unaccountably, a lot of helpers with American accents. The illusion was carefully protected, however, and our Santa was definitely a professional.

'And what do you want for Christmas, young Tom?' he asked after I had introduced the boys to him.

'I sent you a letter,' said Tom rather curtly,

referring to the one that had gone into the wood burner some weeks before and expecting Santa to remember its contents, him being immortal and everything.

'Oh, yes,' said Santa 'it's probably got mixed up on the computer. What did it say?' You had to admire his quick thinking.

Santa and the Ley boys at Selfridges

It was about this time that I discovered evidence of a mouse living in my kitchen. This was very interesting to the boys and to the younger boy Harry in particular. I set a trap and the next morning there was a very dead mouse caught in it. Harry said that he would like to eat it. Where this idea came from I do not know he was generally quite conservative in his tastes. I sent him off to get dressed and removed the unfortunate rodent from the trap and put the little body in the wood burner. By the time Harry had reappeared, I had found a small piece of steak and put it into the frying pan. I explained that I had skinned the mouse and that I would cook it for his breakfast. He readily agreed and ate the morsel fried in olive oil! Years later, in his twenties, he cycled all the way to Beijing, obtained a work permit, found a job as a software engineer and proceeded to join his Chinese hosts in the practice of eating, many things with four legs, as well as quite a lot of things with six legs, eight legs and even things with no legs.

When they were a little older I took them to North Yorkshire for a holiday. We went fishing in the River Tees. Tom had become bored with fishing and was climbing a large rock about three metres high. Harry was considering the mechanics of making his first cast without my help. At just the moment that Tom lost his footing and with a loud wail began sliding down the rock, Harry misjudged his first cast and threw himself full length into the river and sank below the surface, his hair waving gently in the current. Not a good moment for any of us. Tom landed safely, and Harry's swimming lessons had prepared him, so he wasn't too shocked but he was very embarrassed at his state of saturation as we returned to our digs. I asked him what we should tell the landlady.

'Just don't talk about it Dad,' he said anxiously. So I didn't.

With the help of Cecelia, the first girlfriend I went out with after my divorce, I developed the art of quick and easy dessert making. This involved always having to hand ice cream, squirty cream, three types of flavoured syrup, chocolate sprinkles and 'hundreds and thousands.' I encouraged the boys to concoct their own confections. Carefully, Tom read the instructions on the sprinkles container. Under his breath, I heard him say, 'Sprinkle or pour? BOTH,' he shouted as he popped up the two little plastic lids and liberated the contents over his creation. This sums up an attitude to life. Sprinkle or pour? Both. He later became a doctor, paratrooper, and climber.

My wife Valerie was C of E and I had been brought up RC although neither of us were believers. To save arguments between grandmothers, who were believers, we decided not to have our children baptised but to leave it to them, when they were old enough to make an informed decision. One Sunday, the boys and I were visiting my mother at her flat in Bushey, and she asked if we would like to go to church with her. Surprisingly, the boys both wanted to. At the start of the service, the priest called all the small children to the front so that they could be escorted to the church hall by their smiling instructors for Sunday school. Everybody in the congregation was cheered by this charming sight and it was at just this moment, as the joyful group happily left the church, that the twelve-year-old Tom leaned over and mischievously whispered in my ear, 'Is this where they sacrifice all the little children, Dad?'

I had to simulate a coughing fit. Some years later I told this tale to the vicar who married Tom and his fiancée while we were having a quiet drink in a bar in Glasgow the night before the wedding, and he stole it and used it as part of his address at the ceremony.

You can't trust anybody these days, not even a man of the cloth. It was one of my best stories.

After Tom had gone off to university, Harry was staying with me one weekend, and I started a discussion over breakfast. I suggested to him that if there was a God who had created the Universe, then perhaps he had left some clues for us to help prove his existence. We both like science, so I started by suggesting that as the Moon is relatively small and close to the Earth and the Sun is large and far away, it is a very big coincidence that the Moon exactly fits over the Sun during an eclipse. 'Have you noticed anything similar that might be a clue?

'Oh yes,' said the seventeen-year-old Harry,

'fried bacon, it just tastes so good.'
   He might have a point.
   About a year later he, too, went off to University. I do not see them often now as they both live far way. I am proud of the men that they have become, but I do miss my two little boys. I miss them a lot.

Chapter 29 1994 INSIDE BLUNDESTON PRISON

Aged 45

'There's other ways of approaching bank managers guv.'

For reasons with which I will not burden the reader, I found myself, at the age of forty-five, briefly between jobs. Actually, it was not a good time for me, an unexpected divorce followed equally unexpectedly by redundancy was a double whammy. Fortunately, the wife of a friend of mine worked at the education section at Blundeston prison and, with his encouragement, I successfully applied for some part time teaching work. Blundeston was a category B prison in Norfolk. Category A prisons hold terrorists and serial killers, while category B just hold run of the mill criminals, murderers, robbers and the like. I was employed to teach a business course, which was not as unlikely as it sounds because for the previous three years I had been running a computer-aided design agency.

On my first day, I arrived at the entrance to the prison wearing a suit and carrying a large briefcase and announced myself to the gatekeeper as the new teacher. I was taken in and escorted through various levels of security to the education block, surprisingly without being searched or given any advice, or training. Nor, as far as I can remember, did I give any proof of identity.

I was introduced to the head of education at the prison and, after a few welcoming words from him, I took a seat in the tea room waiting, with some trepidation, for the start of my first class. I noticed a female who was standing with her back to me making tea. I assumed that she was another teacher and, being unattached at the time, I waited with interest for her to turn around. When she did I was somewhat shocked at her appearance. She looked rather unfeminine and this was not surprising because 'she' was a transsexual who was part way through the conversion from male to female. She had long hair, makeup and wore false eyelashes. I never did establish how far through the process she was, but she introduced herself as 'Charlie' and asked me if I would like a cup of tea, and I said that I would.

It struck me as rather strange that somebody who was not really fully male should be put into a male prison but then, I suppose, putting her in a female prison would just raise another set of issues. I went into the classroom and introduced myself to the twenty or so inmates and soon afterward Charlie came in with my mug of tea. There were various comments and whistles, which Charlie ignored, like the lady she was. Smiling winningly at me, she placed the mug of tea on my desk and said, 'There you are, Love.' My day was becoming increasingly strange.

'Do you know about Charley, Guv?' asked one of the inmates after she had left the room. I explained that I am always polite to people who are preparing food or drink for me because otherwise you never know what you are eating or drinking, and this raised a laugh. Actually, I never send food back in restaurants, for this reason, although I will complain. Anyway, the inmates were suitably amused, and I felt that the lesson had got off to a good start.

In my classroom there was a big green button mounted on the wall. This was the panic button that I was supposed to press if I suddenly needed the presence of prison officers for whatever reason. I must mention that it was the inmates who told me, with some relish, what it was for, nobody else had mentioned it. As I began my first lesson I found myself not wanting to be far from this button. It was as if I was connected to it by a bungee cord, the further I moved away from it, the stronger the pull back towards it. Eventually, as time passed, I gained some confidence and moved around the classroom normally. My lesson began and the conversation went something like this.

'Well, gentlemen, today we are going to begin the process of preparing a business plan.'

'What's that then Governor?' asks George.

'Well George, it's what you write when you need to approach a bank manager in the hope of getting a loan, perhaps to help you to expand your business. Yes, Harry, what's your question?

'Guv, is this supposed to be like realistic?'

'Yes, Harry, why?'

'Well, because I've turned over three building societies and nobody's going to lend me nothing.' Laughter from the audience and another hand goes up.

'Yes Bill.'

'Well, Guv, I mean, there's other ways of approaching bank managers. You don't need to write all this stuff, you just kidnap their kids.' More knowing laughter and so it went on. It was all very good humoured in a dark sort of way and I found my time in Blundeston prison an education for many reasons.

One day, the subject of 'inflatable girlfriends' came up and several jokes were made. After the lesson, one of the younger inmates chatted with me as the others left. He explained that he was a 'lifer.' This meant that he would be 'inside' for a long time. He explained that he had asked for an 'inflatable girl friend' but had been refused one on the grounds that he might leave it in his bunk with a blanket over it to mask an escape attempt. Actually, there would be no point in him making the request because the press would have had a field day if they had found out that inmates were allowed such things. Many people think that prisoners have an easy enough life already. All I can suggest is that they should try a few nights 'inside,' and see how much they like it.

I later discovered that the young lad that I had been sharing a joke with at the end of my lesson had befriended an elderly man who was in the next bed to him while they were both in hospital. The old chap had told him that he had several gold coins in his flat and invited him to call around for tea so, after they had both been discharged, our young friend and his brother went around to steal the coins. They were discovered by the old man and his wife, so the brothers killed them both with the screwdrivers that they were carrying for that purpose.

He had seemed like such a pleasant, young fellow.

Chapter 30 1997 A CROSSING TO BARDSEY ISLAND

Aged 48

'You can have another mint.'

In the summer of 1997 my two sons and I spent a week of our holiday on the island of Bardsey, a holy island a few miles off the northern Welsh coast. The island of twenty thousand saints. It was a place of pilgrimage in medieval times, where people came to die and be buried in the holy soil. An island, which is almost uninhabited in the winter and during the summer, might have a population of only forty. Bardsey has a diverse and beautiful ecology; wildlife abounds on the island and in the seas, which surround it, although much of the interest seems to centre on sea birds.

In the summer, farmhouses can be rented from the Bardsey Island Trust but if you only need a room or two you can join the group of scientists and amateur ornithologists staying at the Bardsey Bird and Field Observatory. This is a large double fronted 19th century farmhouse called 'Cristin,' where the boys and I had rented a room.

To say that the island lacks services does not fully paint the picture of isolation from the 20th century it represents. Washing water is collected from the roofs in large tanks; drinking water is piped from various springs around the island. There is no shop, though the observatory does keep a supply of essentials. Bread can be a bit of a problem and, in the end, I had to make some myself. If you feel put off by the lack of facilities I can only advise you to go for a day trip. This holiday is for the sort of people who are looking for an escape from too many facilities.

People who want to sit outside at night and see the most amazing sky, unpolluted by street lights. It is for people who want to lie on their back in the grass in the evening and count satellites, while listening to the talk of fellow travellers whose conversational frankness is encouraged by their knowledge that, in a few days time, they will all go their separate ways. People who want to watch birds, talk about birds, ring birds and photograph birds or, in my case, go fishing.

We crossed to Bardsey by boat from the posh marina at Pwllheli on the first morning of our holiday. My boys were both excited at the prospect of a boat trip and of spending a week on an island with all sorts of discoveries to be made. They were ten and eight at the time. The passengers all knew that we would be spending the next week together possibly in close proximity, and I was aware that a lot of polite and unobtrusive 'weighing up' was going on. One of the two boatmen offered round a sweet shop sized jar of Fox's Glacier Mints. Everything seemed very strange after the long road journey, cocooned in our car since we had left Norfolk on the other side of Britain. The feeling of being in a foreign country one minute as the natives talked incomprehensibly in their own language, and the suddenness with which they resolved themselves to be fellow countrymen when they spoke English, was disconcerting, almost like a conjuring trick.

The boat was equipped with a global positioning system to guide us through the fog-shrouded waters. Visibility that morning was barely ten yards. I stood in the cabin behind the 'driver' and enjoyed the technology. The radar warned us of obstacles so we were able to make good time until we were close to the island. On a clear day we would have had sight of it. This time we were sure only that the island was just ahead but where was the quay and the rocks? What of the technology now?

Cautiously, we inched our way towards the shore and eventually the quay appeared out of the mist lined with a dozen or so passengers for the return journey. A few residents had come to meet the boat to collect deliveries of provisions. I noticed that there were three young men working to repair storm damage to the stonework of the quay.

A tractor and trailer took our luggage to Cristin, while we walked the half mile or so along the islands only stony track - there is no metalled road. The boys had loved the boat trip and were now excited as they inspected our room, which was generously supplied with candles and matches. I unpacked our sleeping bags. Electricity is supplied by a generator, which is only started at night, and then only if necessary.

On most of the days that we spent on the island, we managed to go fishing. Actually I'm not very interested in fishing but it is one of those things a father can do with his sons even if he is 'absent' some of the time. Over the years, I have found that two boys each armed with a rod and tackle needs the full-time attention of one adult to continually tie blood knots, bait hooks, cast, untangle line and very occasionally land a fish, while at the time appearing to be only helping a little. If you try to fish with your own rod it all becomes too interrupted and stressful, better to treat it as a spectator sport. When the boys were younger I found that one adult was not really enough. To my mind, fishing is really all about tangle management and trying not to get stabbed with those nasty sharp hooks. Anglers always insist that as they are cold-blooded, fish do not feel pain when they are hooked in the mouth. I think that this is nonsense.

On the first day, after our fishing trip, we visited the Holy Well. I even drank some of the 'healing water' and afterwards I didn't feel any different. I noticed later that there were dead snails floating in the 'healing water', it obviously hadn't done them any good either.

On the second day, we visited the mausoleum of the now dead landowner. This necessitated a tight squeeze through a manhole set in the ground. We continued through a short muddy tunnel with an eventual emergence into a low, brick chamber with a coffin in it. There is no fun to be gained in discovering that you are, after all, slightly claustrophobic while crouching in a small damp room, crowded with people, containing a coffin, with the only exit blocked by a stocky Australian social worker whose legs are the only part of him visible dangling from the roof, and who seems to have got himself stuck in the manhole just when you urgently wanted to leave. It was a bit like being trapped in the engine in Libya years before.

On the same day, we visited the cave of the Hermit, which was nearly as bad. If you are going to get muddy twice, then do it on the same day and save the washing. It was here that my younger son Harry found a perfect crystal of purple quartz.

At nine o'clock each evening at Cristin, a meeting is held to discuss the day's ornithological observations. Both professionals and amateurs gathered around the dining table by the light of a gas lamp, and the warden wrote notes in the logbook. The children's comments were taken as seriously as the adults and this impressed me. At the meeting that evening the lichenologist suggested that Harry's crystal was probably an offering to the Hermit, made by a member of one of the religious sects that periodically stay on the island. One of the Ornithologists asked me if we would be taking the crystal back to the cave to replace it in its nook. Everybody seemed to think that this was the right thing to do except, predictably enough, Harry. It was a bit of a problem for me as Harry had recently developed an interest in geology and was really taken with his new treasure. On the other hand, how would the dead hermit react to the loss of his property? We had a potentially difficult crossing to make back to Pwllheli at the end of our stay: anything could happen. I, of course, am not at all superstitious myself, particularly in daylight and on dry land. The choice here seemed to be between the mystical and the inevitable. I broached the matter obliquely with Harry later.

'What do you think we should do with the crystal?'

'Take it home and put it with my rock collection. We can look it up in the library,' said Harry who was eight. So, no help there then. I decided to put the crystal problem on hold for a bit.

The third day found Tom, Harry and myself practicing jumping across a deep cleft in the ground near the beach. We had already looked at birds from a hide and collected orange and yellow winkle shells, which Harry hoped to use to make a necklace for his mother. I agreed to drill holes in them for him when we returned home. As we happily jumped over successively wider parts of the cleft and discussed jumping techniques, the stocky Australian social worker, James, appeared and joined in. We had got to know him quite well and enjoyed his sense of humour and his attempts at naive water colouring, which he did in a school exercise book. Tom jumped and gave a cry as he landed, twisting his ankle in the process. He lay on the ground, grimacing with pain. Tom seldom makes a fuss but on this occasion he was verging on tears. I was slightly worried that he might have a fracture. Our relative isolation compounded my concern. I sat down on the ground next to Tom, gently removed his shoe and sock and examined his ankle. Everything seemed all right, there was no swelling or bruising, his foot was not hanging unnaturally. I became aware of James talking to Tom behind me.

'How do you feel about your injury Tom? Have you had the chance to talk to anybody about your feelings? Do you think your father is concentrating too much on the physical aspect and not being holistic enough?' He was sitting cross-legged on the ground at Tom's shoulder paying close attention to him while simultaneously rolling a cigarette. Even Tom found it funny.

On the fourth day, I ate fresh lobster with my first loaf of home-made bread. I was surprised at how easy bread-making is. You basically add water to a powder, mix it up, and go fishing, and when you get back, put it in the oven for a bit. I had never eaten fresh lobster before and so I had treated myself to one that had been caught that day. As I was about to put the live lobster into the pan of boiling water, I discovered that nearly everybody staying at the observatory was firstly, in the kitchen, and secondly, a vegetarian. I stood by one of the two cooking stoves indecisively clutching in one hand the unfortunate crustacean, which was slowly waving claws held shut by elastic bands, and in the other hand, the lid of the steaming saucepan. I was surrounded by politely disapproving but fascinated onlookers, who had all mysteriously congregated to make bean salads or peanut butter sandwiches at this precise moment. Frankly, I felt like an executioner which I suppose, in truth, I was. Would the lobster let out a blood-curdling scream as it sank into the scalding depths? I felt guilty then, and I feel guilty now writing about it, but I was not going to put that lobster back into the 'briny.' I had been looking forward to this meal. A young biology teacher came to my rescue.

A meal of homemade beer, homemade bread and lobster with James outside Cristin

'The lobster will only last for a couple of seconds in boiling water,' he said, his biological knowledge adding weight to his opinion. Everybody relaxed visibly and watched with fascination as I thrust the lobster into the pot. We all hoped that the banging and clanking, which we heard subsequently was the boiling water rattling it against the sides of the pan. The vegetarians carried on making their peanut butter sandwiches.

The other residents at Cristin were a varied bunch. I have already mentioned the social worker and the lichenologist. The bird photographer was a tanned and rugged individual who lived on tinned stew. He tried tinned chilli one day because we continually bullied him about the lack of variety in his diet, but he clearly regretted it and went back to his original dish. This was a man heedless of frivolities such as dietary variety, a man truly dedicated to his art, whose fascination with bird life put even twitchers in the shade. A man who had recently spent three months by himself in a tent on the Canadian tundra, attempting to photograph a small brown bird, whose name escapes me, and living, inevitably, on tinned stew. By the end of the week I had grown to admire his patience and self-sufficiency. Apparently, tinned stew contains every nutrient that is necessary to sustain human life. I wonder if NASA knows about this. They might find it useful for any future mission to Mars.

There was a musical evening. The first event was Morris dancing by six people, only one of whom knew how to do it. We might have needed to call out the helicopter from the mainland to fly the injured back to hospital, given the enthusiasm with which the dancers wielded their sticks. Teaching people to Morris dance is a great way to break the ice at the sober beginning of parties, but you should on no account try it at the end of the evening. I sang the blues, the other English guitarist sang Irish songs, but the three Welsh people said that they couldn't sing. Now that's a turn up for the book, I thought, and went back to the observatory for fresh supplies of beer. It turned out that these people could only not sing when they were sober. In the end they sang a really soulful hymn called 'Sosban bach.' which, when sung slowly and sadly in Welsh, brought tears to my eyes. You have to picture the group of singers gathered on the hillside, the sunset and the sea birds calling as they sang the 'song of their fathers.'

It turns out that the song is a catalogue of comic mishaps concerning a saucepan boiling over, somebody with their shirt hanging out, a baby crying and a dog which has just bitten little Johnny. I had always thought it was a hymn until it was translated for me.

At the end of the holiday we prepared for the journey home, and walked half a mile to the quay, our bags going ahead by tractor and trailer. I was walking behind Tom and Harry. Some twenty-five yards ahead of me I saw Harry pause and scan the ground. When I caught up with him he told me that he had dropped his crystal on the track. He was puzzled that he could not find it. It was almost as if it had disappeared as it hit the ground, he told me.

'Leave it, Harry,' I said gently. He shrugged, I put my hand on his shoulder and we walked on towards the boat. He didn't seem to mind losing the crystal too much really. I sometimes wonder if we might find it again if we looked in its nook in the hermit's cave.

Eventually, when all were aboard, the boat set off on the forty-five minute journey back to the twentieth century. This time, all the passengers knew each other and the atmosphere was much more relaxed than it had been on the way out. Activity holidays are a very good way of meeting people, especially if you are single and we had all got on well together at Cristin. As we set off, the boatman came around with the Fox's Glacier Mints again and we all laughed at a familiar joke. The boat moved further from Bardsey, across the sound, but at right angles to our course, I saw a red flare at sea level a mile or two away. Quickly, I went to the cabin at the front of the boat where the crew of two had not yet spotted it. I pointed it out to them. It could have been a light on a buoy but the long trail of smoke blown away from it by the wind was the clincher. There was sudden excitement as the boat altered course. Our mint-offering boatswain suddenly came over all official as he informed the coastguard of the flare by VHF radio. You don't get the chance to be involved in a rescue every day, but all three of us were probably a little worried that it might be a false alarm with consequent embarrassment to follow.

Some minutes later, we drew level with a small motorboat containing three embarrassed young men. To say that their boat had seen better days might be the kindest way to describe it. The three young men were the masons who had been repairing the quay on Bardsey when we first arrived. Every morning, they would cross the sound in their small craft to do their day's work, and every evening they would cross back. This morning the engine had failed half way across the sound. The boat had drifted closer and closer to the rocks where it would have been smashed to pieces, and they had taken turns to sit with one leg over the side of the boat, one to port and one to starboard, paddling furiously with their builders shovels, for they had no oars. They had been in this predicament for over an hour and were obviously glad to have been rescued, but one could not help feeling that they would have preferred to have been rescued less publicly, for it rather spoilt the image of tanned and tattooed independence that they had projected all week down at the quay on Bardsey.

We towed the motor boat across to the mainland and the young men cast off while we were still a hundred metres from the shore. I watched them paddle away with their shovels and wondered just how much 'stick' they were going to have to take at their local pub that week. Our boat put on speed and headed towards Pwllheli once again. I went forward to the cabin. The boatmen were discussing the incident in Welsh, and politely and probably unconsciously, shifted seamlessly into English as I joined them. The one 'driving' congratulated me on my observation of the flare.

'Well done for that,' he said turning around as he spoke to me.

'I expect to be made an honorary Welshman now,' I said. No response, but a slightly suspicious look. Was I being facetious? 'Or at least be given the freedom of Pwllheli.' I was being facetious. There was a pause.

'You can 'ave another mint,' he said rather shortly

and returned his attention to the view forward.

I had to get it myself, so I took two while he wasn't looking.

Chapter 31 2006 DOING SOMETHING SLIGHTLY DANGEROUS

Aged 57

'Welcome to Ireland.'

It was the Easter holiday and I had gone to Dublin by myself for a few days. My wife was not able to come because she was caring for her mother, whose great age was beginning to get the better of her. I found the business of staying in a hotel by myself and taking solitary trips around Dublin rather lonely, but I made the best of it. My first excursion was on the tour bus around the city. This is usually a good way to start to a city break type of holiday: it helps you to get your bearings.

As we drove around the city I was impressed by the humorous chat that the bus driver gave over the public address system. As I left the bus I complimented him on his witty delivery. He seemed pleased and gave the impression that he was only driving the bus to pay the bills, and that he hoped for better things, possibly in the entertainment industry, in the future. The next day, I got onto another bus (the ticket was valid for twenty four hours) and was regaled with the same 'spontaneous' humour from a different driver who told exactly the same jokes. As a lecturer, I always hated it when students had to repeat a year on my engineering courses for the same reason of repetitions.

I got off the bus at the Irish museum of Modern Art for want of anything better to do, and spent a pleasant hour looking at the exhibits. It was at this point, as I was leaving the museum at around lunchtime, that I noticed some posters advertising the 'AutoCAD dealers of Ireland Conference.' Now AutoCAD is a famous computer-aided design package and it so happens that some years before, I had been an AutoCAD dealer myself, back in Gt Yarmouth, when I had taken a stint out of teaching and run a CAD bureau. The conference was having its lunch break and I could see through an open door that it consisted of a very appetising-looking buffet. I suddenly felt that AutoCAD inc could probably afford to buy me a meal, and anyway, there is always too much food provided at this sort of event.

I weighed up the pros and cons. If I was not found out, I would have a delicious meal. If I was found out, I would be ejected and suffer humiliation, but I doubted that the organisers would call the police and have me arrested. On the other hand, they might. It probably wouldn't be as scary as when I was arrested in Tripoli. The Garda Siochana tends not to point machine guns at you under these circumstances.

I thought back to one of the lecturers at Nottingham University, where I had trained for my teaching qualification. As a young man, he had felt himself to be too cautious and as part of his self-education had made himself take bus journeys without paying for the ticket. He had felt that it was a victimless crime and it made him feel better about himself.

I made up my mind to follow his example and walked into the conference and took a place in the queue at the buffet. I looked the serving staff straight in the eye, smiled, cracked the odd joke, accepted a glass of red wine and took a table close to the wall, in the hope that nobody noticed the lack of an identity badge pinned to my lapel.

I felt slightly stressed and probably didn't enjoy the meal as much as I would if I had been there with permission, but as I was leaving with a very nice pudding and a couple of glasses of wine inside me, I felt like a new man, a dangerous man, a daring man, a devil-may-care fellow who could live off his wits.

A member of the conference staff, a young chap, pressed a leaflet into my hand at the doorway, and I found myself thanking him for the fine meal I just eaten. He looked at my lapel and, probably noticed my lack of a badge, paused as he looked at me for a moment considering his response.

'Well welcome to Ireland,' he said agreeably.

But I'm not sure what he was thinking.

Roger Ley

PART FOUR RETIREMENT

And remarriage

Chapter 32   2008 THE AUTOCAD DIARIES

Aged 59

'Are we learning yet?'

When my children were quite small the family went on holiday to Scotland. The weather was good, and we had sunshine every day. In the mornings, I would sit in the sun for an hour by myself and read the AutoCAD software manual.

I should explain that AutoCAD is an internationally well known computer-aided design package and it was my intention to learn how to use it, so that I could teach it at Lowestoft College, where I was a lecturer. At that time, CAD was coming into engineering in much the same way that word processing had taken over from typing a few years before. I could see that drawing boards would soon be replaced by computer screens, in much the same way that typewriters had been replaced by word processors.

My wife, Valerie, was not keen on my morning breaks for study and accused me of spoiling the holiday. I pointed out that all I had brought along was the AutoCAD manual while she had brought her mother. An uneasy truce ensued.

As it happens, I finished reading the manual, learned the software and made a good living from AutoCAD for the next twenty-five years and found it very interesting and absorbing. Taking up CAD was one of my better decisions in life.

During the last few years of my working life, I was a Senior Lecturer in the Engineering department at City College Norwich. I loved the work and generally liked the students. When they get to sixteen, they stop telling their parents if you use the odd 'Anglo-Saxon' word in a lesson. They were often really funny and they kept me up to date with new ideas like Facebook and YouTube. I taught a lot of AutoCAD. Soon after the lesson began and the students had fired up their computers and started working, I would loudly ask the all important question.

'Are we learning yet?'

The students would call back either, 'Yes' or 'No' depending on their mood at the time.

I would often stress the importance of referring to the AutoCAD manual, which was about as big as an encyclopaedia. In order to reinforce this advice and to try to get my students to refer to it themselves I found myself making up a story about how the AutoCAD manual had saved my life on one occasion, and, eventually, by popular demand it became a feature of the lesson. I would tell them a tall story about how the manual had saved my life, or I had saved other peoples with its help. I hasten to add that the stories were briefly told, while the students were busy working on their drawing projects. I found that they worked more quietly at such times because they wanted to hear what I had to say. I would walk around the class inspecting their work and giving suggestions, but they were always listening and tried to catch me out on the details.

I told them how the AutoCAD manual had first saved my life when I was working in the Libyan Desert. I had been walking around a sand dune, when I was confronted by an Egyptian soldier who raised his rifle and shot at me. I happened to have the manual with me and I instinctively held it up, and it stopped the bullet. Somebody would often ask how far the bullet had penetrated, so at this point I would pick up a manual and open it at random and quote whatever page number and main heading I found myself looking at. For instance, 'Page six hundred and fifty four, 'Working with Drawings and External References Productively.'" The story did not take into account the fact that personal computers had not been invented at the time that I was referring to, and what was I doing with an AutoCAD manual in the Libyan Desert anyway?

One of my students asked what had happened to the manual and I told him that I had used it to beat the Egyptian soldier into submission and had kept it and the bullet as souvenirs. I promised to bring them both to the next lesson but unaccountably would always forget. The best of it was that, as I was teaching the same course to four different groups of students, I was able to polish the stories as the week went on.

The next story soon hatched with very little incubation on my part. This time, I was a passenger on a Jumbo Jet on a trans-Atlantic flight when both pilots fell ill and the senior flight attendant called over the public address system, in a panic-stricken voice, 'Are there any pilots on board?' Needless to say I stepped forward, and with the help of the AutoCAD manual to operate all the throttles at the same time, I landed the plane safely. I am afraid that this reflects one of my recurring fantasies. You may recall that I had ten hours of pilot training on light aircraft nearly fifty years ago. How difficult can it be to land a Jumbo Jet?

'It wasn't the best landing that I ever made,' I would say with careless bravado to the waiting press, 'but any landing that you can walk away from is a landing, not a crash.' Only when the students insisted on additional details, did I mention the fact that, at the time, I was being carried on the shoulders of the grateful passengers while the flight attendants gazed adoringly up at me.

The stories got more outrageous. The aircraft scenario was so popular that I was able to use the manual to good effect on other flights. I used it to cover a hole made by a hijacker's hand grenade to save the plane from depressurisation. It also plugged the ventilation system when a number of snakes escaped from their crate in the hold. You may recognise that last scenario. I had run out of ideas so, I had engaged one of my day release groups to come up with unlikely stories to tell to the full-time engineering students. That is how the last one slipped in, I had not heard of the film 'Snakes on a Plane' at the time.

Moving away from aircraft, there was the occasion that I was leading a group of Royal Marine Commandos on a mountaineering expedition, and the weather changed suddenly. We were trapped high up in the Alps, wet, cold, hungry, and just as they were giving up hope and breaking down in tears, I saved the day by using the trusty manual to sledge down the mountain side at great risk to myself, and was able to alert a group of Paratroopers, who were able to scale the mountain and carry them back down.

I must explain that my older son is a Paratrooper in the Army Reserves. If he had been a Marine I would have told the story the other way around to retain family honour. I should mention that the Marines work for the Royal Navy and the Paratroopers are in the British Army and there is more than an element of rivalry between them.

On one occasion, I recounted how I had been forced to eat a copy of the manual, five pages per day, in order to stay alive, when I was parachuted into the jungle to lead a group of Special Forces personnel out, after they became lost. This accounted for my uncannily thorough knowledge of the AutoCAD software. I had digested all of it except for the section on printing drawings because that is covered in the last chapter and I had rescued the group before I consumed it.

In every case, the AutoCAD manual bore the scars of its adventures and it was a shame that I could never remember to bring it in to show the students.

Then, one day, the new Principal arrived to take over the College. He introduced a policy of continuous internal inspection by people who had no knowledge of the subject that they were inspecting; they were rather like a Gestapo unit going around striking dread in the hearts of fully competent and indeed valuable teaching staff. Teaching became all about grades, tick boxes and 'education speak.' I do believe in thorough lesson preparation and in high-quality teaching, but there has to be room for a bit of fun, now and again. The inspections were harsh and unsupportive, designed to undermine people and quite a lot of staff left, unable to cope. One month, nine teachers resigned from the engineering department.

On one of my inspections, I was teaching 3-Dimensional Design and Rapid Prototyping to a group of mature male students. The inspection report allowed that I knew my subject, (although how the young Arts graduate who was inspecting me would know is a mystery); she observed that because the group were all 'boys,' (some of them were in their forties), they would be too nervous to ask questions, and I should issue each of them with a little set of 'traffic lights' so that they could signal to me whether or not they were understanding the lesson - she obviously came from a background of primary education. The students, whose employers were paying hefty fees, would have been insulted, and how I would have explained this nonsense to an irate employer if one phoned me about it, I do not know. I remembered the words of my boss, Frank Cox, when I had worked offshore thirty years before. I had asked him why he had retired from the Royal Navy.

'When the gentlemen left the Navy, so did I,' said Frank.

At the age of sixty-one, and with the feeling, that the barbarians had taken over Further Education, I decided that, sadly, it was time for me to leave. I had no wish to grow a beard. (Barbarian means 'bearded one' in Latin - but you knew that!)

As a leaving present, the National Diploma class were kind enough to present me with a copy of the AutoCAD manual, which had a bullet hole, blood, four 747 throttle handle indentations and sledge marks. They also set up a Facebook page called 'Roger Ley the best teacher ever at Norwich City College.'

This may have been a slight over-statement. But it was certainly nice to leave on a high note.

N D Eng 2 presents me with a battle-scarred AutoCAD manual as a leaving gift.

Chapter 33   2009 THE PARK INN HOTEL IN BERLIN

Aged 60

'I hope that you enjoyed your stay, mein Herr.'

Recently, my wife and I spent a city break in Berlin. We stayed at the Park Inn in Alexanderplatz, and very nice it was too. The hotel was about thirty storeys high and our room was about half way up. We arrived in the afternoon, feeling rather tired after our flight from Stansted. We were booked in by a young, male concierge with a rather formal demeanour. He stood almost at attention as he spoke to us. Having found our room, we decided to lie down and rest for ten minutes before starting our exploration of the city. As I lay on the bed with my eyes partly closed, I thought I saw a shadow pass across the window which looked over Alexanderplatz towards the landmark television tower. Probably a bird I thought, a seagull perhaps, something quite large anyway. As I lay half asleep the same thing happened again, but this time there seemed to be a faint cry coming through the double glazed sliding doors to the balcony. My wife had not noticed anything as she was facing the wrong way.

Unable to rest I got up, opened the sliding doors and went out onto the balcony to investigate, just as a human body fell screaming past me towards the square below. I was appalled and looking over the balcony, was in time to see the victim being safely decelerated to a stop just a few metres above the ground by the cable to which he was attached. They were 'base jumping,' I looked up and could see that there was a concession on the roof, presumably with the requisite helmets, cables, harnesses and braking system.

Once we understood what was happening we became quite used to it. It happened for a short time each day, it was only the people laughing loudly as they went down that unsettled me.

The Park Inn in Berlin, the base jumping concession is at the top

Unaccountably, my wife felt no urge to have a go, no matter how much I encouraged her. I would have liked to have a go myself, but I suffer from an excess of good sense when it comes to fairground rides and the like.

At the end of our stay we checked out at the front desk and, coincidentally, the same somewhat reserved concierge dealt with us.

'I hope that you enjoyed your stay, mein Herr,' he said somewhat stiffly as I operated the credit card machine.

'Well, actually, it would have been nice, when we checked in, if you had warned us about the base jumpers falling past our balcony,' I said.

He paused, considered for a moment, looked at me and I saw the barest flicker of a smile appear on one side of his mouth.

'Ja,' he said in excellent but slightly accented English, 'perhaps ve should varn people in ze future.'

I knew that he wouldn't though.

Chapter 34 2011 FILMING 'A MOTHER'S SON'

Aged 62

Standing in

As everybody knows, teaching is the 'last refuge of a scoundrel', so when I retired from it at the age of sixty, I was left with few sanctuaries. As a means of diversion I joined an amateur dramatics society, little realising that the term 'amateur dramatics' largely refers to the antics of the members of the society off stage rather than their performances on it. Some of the members took their talents seriously enough to have joined a local theatrical agency and had secured work as extras when film and television companies were working in our area. I live near Southwold in Suffolk, which is suitably rural and picturesque, but a relatively short trip up the A12 from London, so it is popular with these companies for filming in the summer.

One of our older members had previously spent two days as an extra, filming with a well-known actress, who was naked for the whole of the two days that it took to complete one scene. It certainly put a spring in his septuagenarian step; he told me all about it several times, and actually he told everybody he met about it several times. Why the film company bothered to pay him I do not know.

Unexpectedly, soon after I had registered with the agency I received an urgent call: I was to be available for two days filming in Southwold, starting the next day - somebody had dropped out. It was not until I arrived on the common near the water towers where the film company was encamped, that I found out that I was to play the part of a policeman. Not a 'plain clothes' policeman, but a real policeman with a uniform, a truncheon, a helmet and even a pepper spray (filled with water.) I could not believe my good fortune. They were going to, feed me, with very good food, and pay me £100 per day to dress as a policeman and swan around Southwold. It sounded nearly as good as my first job fifty years before when I had worked on the film with Tony Hancock and had been given money and unlimited quantities of ice cream.

The drama in question was 'A Mother's son' with Martin Clunes, Hermione Norris and Paul McGann. Hermione Norris was present on the second day and she seemed very pleasant and quiet, but I didn't have the pleasure of the company of the other two. Never mind, I am not really keen on the current obsession with celebrity. I am always annoyed, for instance, when political parties 'wheel out' actors to support them at election time. Why would I want to know about their opinions - they are only actors, for God's sake? What do they know about fiscal theory or foreign relations? Unless, of course, political theory is part of the syllabus at RADA, and I just hadn't realised it.

There were a couple of dozen of us bogus police constables on the set, and I noticed an interesting phenomenon. There was a tendency to 'clump.' If a couple of policemen went into the tea hut, then gradually we all went in. If several of us left, the rest soon followed. The actor Charleton Heston observed, when filming 'The Planet of the Apes,' that initially, at meal breaks, the chimps, gorillas and orang-utans all sat at mixed tables but after a few days they unconsciously segregated themselves, the chimps sat with chimps, the orang-utans with orang-utans. Mind you he was, for a time, the president of the National Rifle Association of America and held some pretty right wing views. I always felt that his story contained a hint of racism.

Filming in Southwold

I am afraid that the opportunity to uniform myself as a policeman brought out both the best and the worst in me. One of my co-workers observed that I had, 'Even started to walk like a copper.'

'Oh really,' I said as I put my thumbs in the top pockets of my tunic, raised myself up on tiptoe and then flexed my knees.

The people of Southwold seemed oblivious to the fact that we were actors, and seemed to assume that we were there in a professional capacity to help the film crew with traffic and crowd control. As I stood next to an extra who was playing the part of a passerby, I noticed a builder's wagon driving slowly past, the young driver leaning out to see what was going on. For no particular reason, I pointed sternly at him, he blanched and hurriedly did up his seat belt. My companion was very amused and asked me whether or not I was a method actor.

Later, my next door neighbour walked past and I had the great satisfaction of approaching him from behind, placing my hand on his shoulder and saying sonorously,

'You are under arrest.' The effect was most gratifying. He has never forgiven me.

My now retired ex-head of department from Norwich City College approached me from among the passing shoppers and said, somewhat breathlessly, 'I thought that it was you. Is this what you do now?'

'Yes,' I said, although I do not know whether he thought that I was an actor or a policeman. Uniforms are surprisingly powerful things. I hate to think of what you could get away with if you put your mind to it, had access to good theatrical costumiers, and were not afraid of the consequences.

The best part was at the end of the second day, when the extras were getting their notes signed so that they could claim for the day's work. A group of them were rather ancient and were waiting to cross the busy main street in Southwold. Seizing the opportunity, I stepped into the road, held up my hand, stopped the traffic, motioned the pedestrians across and then waved the traffic on. How satisfying. In the setting of Southwold it seemed to me to be just the way the world ought to be, a sunny day at the coast and a friendly policeman helping old people across the road, it was a perfect end to a perfect day. My only regret is that, during the two days of filming, there was never an opportunity for me to chase somebody down the street, blowing my whistle loudly and waving my truncheon.

Next time perhaps.

Chapter 35   2012 THE HORSE IN THE MORNING

Aged 63

I live in a fairly ordinary bungalow in rural Suffolk between Framlingham and Saxmundham. My house is separated from our single track village road by a steep concrete drive about twenty five yards long.

One summer morning at about eight o'clock I heard a strange noise at my front door. It was not a conventional knock but definitely some sort of signal. I got up to investigate and as I walked down my hallway, I was surprised to see what appeared to be a horse's head framed in the large glass pane of my front door. With some mystification, I opened the door to see who had come to see me on horseback and, more to the point, why? Perhaps they wanted to use my phone or needed some other sort of help.

Stepping out of the door, I found a large chestnut horse standing quietly by my step with no rider, saddle or harness. It had walked up my drive from the road and was standing there quietly almost as if it was expected. It had tapped at the bottom of my door with the front of one hoof, as horses do when they are confined to a stable and want to attract attention.

My equine visitor

      I did not have the first idea what to do. I found a bucket and put some water in it and offered it to my visitor, but after a cursory sniff it didn't seem interested. I didn't have any suitable food so I chatted to it about this and that as I stroked and patted its shoulder. I continued to talk in a soothing manner but the horse was very calm and untroubled. I felt very much at peace myself as I stood in the morning sunshine and felt myself forming a strong bond with this lovely, powerful, yet gentle animal. It began to stare through my large front window and seemed very interested in the contents of my lounge. I stood undecidedly wondering what to do. The horse continued its critical appraisal of my new leather sofas. In the end, I came to a decision and rang my neighbour (no pun intended). Well, he is a farmer and he jolly well ought to know what to do in this situation. Eventually, he came, took a look and then rang a woman he knew, who keeps horses about a quarter of a mile away. Some twenty minutes later she arrived with a stable hand; they put a bridle on the horse and quietly took it away. Apparently, later, the owner came to retrieve it, and I never saw it again.

I found out later that day that the horse had escaped from its field about twelve miles away, earlier that morning. When the owner discovered that it was missing she had alerted the police and Radio Suffolk. The horse was seen to have galloped through several villages and to have crossed the busy A12 dual carriageway, luckily without mishap. The radio station reported this county-wide but nobody could catch it; dealing with big strong animals like horses is a skill long lost to most of us and, anyway, who walks around with a handy piece of rope in their hand these days?

As to its strange behaviour after its arrival, apparently the horse had not been interested in my lounge, just its own reflection in the window. It had probably never seen a mirror before and thought that there was another horse in there. It could not see the window from the road though, so that is not what attracted it in the first place: possibly my house looked familiar to it? I still wonder why it didn't choose one of the many open field entrances on its route and go in and eat grass as you would expect a horse to do.

It had been a very unusual experience. It is not everybody who has to answer their door first thing in the morning to a polite knock, and find a friendly, rider-less horse on the doorstep, looking for all the world like the children's television character, Mister Ed.

It might have happened to anybody, I suppose, but I am still left wondering why it chose my house of all the houses along its route, and why it was so composed when it arrived. It still seems strange as I think about it now a year later: could this be a fourth unexplained event along with the Djinn, the Girl on the Underground and the Dowsing?

When Ann arrived home later I told her about

the horse and explained my mystification and strange attachment to it. She asked me whether it had been male or female. I said that I hadn't looked.

'No,' she said nodding understandingly, 'you're right, not on a first date,' and laughed quietly to herself as she hung her coat up.

Chapter 36   2014 ELECTRIC SHADOWS

Aged 65

'You seem a little surprised Harry.'

My son Harry who was now twenty-seven-years old had spent several months cycling from the UK to Beijing and taken a job as a software engineer there. It had been a rather worrying time for me - I wondered how safe it was for him to camp in wild areas and on the side of the road in Siberia, Mongolia and the Gobi desert. I found that I needed to have my mobile phone with me ALL the time in case he rang me needing help. Although what I could have done if he was in trouble in the Gobi desert, I do not know. Hire a helicopter perhaps? After he had been settled in Beijing for about six months, and I had not seen him for a year, I flew out both to see him and to have an adventure of my own in China.

Harry met me at the airport when I arrived, and, after a bit of manly hugging and back slapping, we took a taxi to the centre of Beijing. It felt very strange to hear my son confidently speaking Mandarin to the taxi driver. Beijing seemed so alien to me, but Harry took it all in his stride; I was slightly in awe of him. Suddenly, he was looking after me, rather than vice versa. He wanted to tell him which things seemed strange to me in China as he had been there long enough to become used to it all. Which things? Well, everything actually.

The plan was that we would spend a few days together seeing the sights in Beijing, and then I would move on by myself to Xian (pronounced Sheean) to see the Terracotta Army. After this, we would meet up in Hong Kong and he would show me around the ex-colony for a few days before I flew back home to the

UK.

After I had checked into my hotel, we set off on foot towards Tiananmen Square. Bicycles and eerily silent electric scooters come at us from all directions. Later I found that the best way to cross the street was to shadow a local person. They seemed to understand and sympathise with my perplexity. Harry observed that the Chinese cyclists should oil their chains more often. Well, he would notice things like that after cycling all the way from England to China. You don't get far without oiling your chain you know!

We went to the Forbidden City and sat for a while outside a nice little cafe and drank 'three-in-one coffee,' which is instant coffee with milk and sugar added, whether you like it or not - I did. Harry told me more of his adventures cycling over the mountains to Beijing, and how cold the wild camping was. He used to cook pasta and then use the pasta water to make tea - apparently it's delicious if you are on the verge of hypothermia. I was so glad that he had kept his 'on the road' emails to me 'upbeat'. One day, I am sure that he will tell me about some of the more exciting adventures that he had on his odyssey; hopefully, we will be sitting safely by a nice log fire, in my front room drinking a glass of whiskey.

Llama temple roof detail all the figures mean something in Chinese folklore

That afternoon, we went to Jingshan Park and Pavilion, which gives a wonderful view over the Forbidden City, another huge statement of power by the Emperor of the time. The weather was peachy, the air quality was fairly good, and, as we walked back, we bought some grapes dipped in melted sugar and impaled on a sliver of bamboo from a street vendor with a tricycle fitted out as a mobile stall. The vendor wanted 50 pence. Outrageous. Harry bargained competently, as was expected of him, but the confectioner was surprisingly unrelenting, so in the end we paid up and unexpectedly he gave us an extra stick of grapes. I think that he was being friendly but here may have been a misunderstanding about how many sticks we were bidding for.

Over the next couple of days, as Harry and I went about the city, I picked up the usual few words that a traveller needs in a foreign country, but one that was surprisingly useful was the word 'Laoren' which means 'old person' or 'pensioner,' which combined with the presentation of my bus pass at the ticket window, sometimes got me into venues at half price. At other times, the official would impatiently tell Harry that only Chinese pensioners qualify for the reduction. I would point at my bus pass in an attempt to make them think that it had some official capacity in the Peoples Republic of China, but the Suffolk County Council logo wasn't fooling anybody.

A street musician in Beijing

    We went to the Summer Palace, which has a lovely long walk with lakes, pagodas, families (one child only), gardens, specially imported rocky outcrops and the Long Corridor, which is a roofed walk that the Emperor could use in inclement weather. It was highly decorated and colourful. After an hour, we sat on the grass for a snack, and I started to peel a banana. Harry observed that I had opened it from the wrong end. I tried opening it from the other end, and he was right: it is easier. Try it next time you eat one. You can imagine my confusion as I contemplated the previous sixty-five-years years of erroneous banana peeling. I didn't know what to say, we looked at each other in silent embarrassment; in the end, to break the uncomfortable silence, I asked him how he had discovered this.

'Monkeys always open them from that end,' he said and continued to look at me. Although he didn't actually say anything, I knew that in his mind there was a silent comparison being made between me and a chimpanzee, and I wasn't coming out of it well.

That afternoon we went to a market, but it was too exhausting for me to feel like buying anything. There was too much eagerness to make a sale, too much haggling. One punter seriously annoyed a stall holder,

'Very ugly,' she called at the putative customer's retreating back. 'VERY UGLY!' she shouted as the distance increased. Harry told me that Chinese people are usually less demonstrative than this; she must have been seriously annoyed.

One evening, we went to have dinner at one of Harry's regular restaurants. For years, he has been an enthusiastic player of the oriental board game called 'Go', and this was a place that his Go club retired to at the end of their evening sessions. It was reassuringly full of locals enjoying beautifully presented food in a slightly 'down-at-heel' environment. The ambiance was just right: the food had lots of chilli and numbing spice. There was mutton, pork, prawns and vegetables. Rice was served last as an afterthought, in case the main courses were not enough. The numbing spice was a strange, new experience. It raised the question why would you want to eat something that numbed your lips and mouth? It was all very mainland Chinese, and nothing like the Cantonese food that we are used to in the UK.

'Ganbei,' (empty glass) we said in unison as we clinked our glasses together and then downed our beer. Small glasses, of course, to allow for many refills. Displaying the correct Chinese etiquette, Harry kept his glass lower than mine - I am after all, the senior family member, and good manners cost nothing!

After a few days in Beijing, I set off by myself on the 200 mph bullet train to the city of Xian to see the Terracotta Army. I had a wonderful time in the Muslim quarter that evening. Even the babies wore prayer hats. Harry called me from Beijing on the mobile phone that he had lent to me, to see if I was alright.

'Of course I am, Harry,' I said, 'what could possibly go wrong?'

On the way home, I saw couples ballroom dancing in the park, ladies doing tai chi, and, best of all, men energetically whipping big wooden spinning tops. 'Crack, crack' - serious, shirt-off, manly stuff. Gesturing, I asked if I could take a photograph.

'Have a go,' the Chinese man responded. 'Have a good crack at it.' So I did, and he took a picture of me. It was really good fun.

A Horse in the Morning

Whipping a spinning top in the park in Xian, really good fun

I went back to the hotel to write my email home and to have a drop of 'Peoples Republic Rocket Fuel,' imported direct from the launch sites at Jiuquan and bottled locally.

It was surprisingly good, but, 'Don't smoke at the same time comrade,' it said on the bottle.

No, it didn't, I have no idea what it said on the bottle, it was all in Chinese characters.

Two days later, Harry and I met up in Hong Kong. I thought that it was so nice of him to give up part of his annual holiday and to fly there to show me around. It truly is a wonderful place and very different from the mainland. I had asked to go walking in the New Territories, so we took a bus to the Tai Po Kau nature reserve, which seemed to have been designed by Escher in that it has a circular seven-mile hike, apparently uphill all the way around (not possible if you think about it), and it was very hot; we drank two litres of water each during this outing. After about an hour of walking Harry, who was a pace ahead of me, suddenly jumped in the air and shouted,

'Aaaaaaargh.' On the ground at his feet was a black Chinese Cobra about a metre long and as thick as my forearm. It hissed loudly, rearing up and raising its hood. I immediately pushed Harry out of danger, quickly grabbed it by the tail, cracked it like a whip to break its neck, and we took it back to a local restaurant, where the chef was happy to cook it for our evening meal accompanied by a nice Chianti. Well, again actually that isn't quite what happened - I sprang up onto a large rock, and Harry had also jumped out of the way rather quickly.

'You seem a little surprised, Harry,' I said attempting to be casual about the most frightening thing that had happened to me since I was charged by an elephant at the age of fifteen, or possibly when I made my first solo air flight a couple of years later.

We watched as the Cobra took its grumpy time slithering away under a boulder. Presumably it had decided that we were too big to eat, and so, not worth fighting. As we continued our walk after this, every tree root looked suspicious to me. I made sure that Harry took the lead for the rest of the walk. Later we had a laugh about it.

'Ha ha,' we said unconvincingly in our hotel room. 'Ha ha ha.' And we opened another bottle of beer.

That evening Harry told me that the biggest insult that you can give to a Cantonese person is to call them a 'Turtle egg.' We couldn't work out why, so, as an experiment, Harry decided to call me random things to see what effect they had. He called me, 'A suitcase.' - I must say that I didn't feel good about it, but at least he hadn't called me a Turtle egg.

We talked about the Mandarin language and its reliance on tones. We use them a bit in English, for instance, at the end of a question we use a rising inflection. Australians do it at the end of every sentence.

Mandarin has four different tones. Harry told me that in Mandarin 'films' translates as 'electric shadows.' We both liked that.

The next day, I flew back to the UK. I was not too troubled about leaving Harry in China as I knew that he would be coming home for Christmas in a few months. He did a wonderful job of navigating us around Beijing and Hong Kong on busses, taxis and subways. It was a privilege to join him on his big adventure, even if only for a couple of weeks.

As I write this chapter he has been back home, but then he left a month later. He travelled around New Zealand for a few months, and then took a job in Australia. When he emailed to me that he had been successful in his job application, I sent an email saying, 'Great news on my impending holiday in Australia.' I am not sure when I will see him again, but, until then, there's always Skype.

He is talking about South America soon. I can hardly wait.

Chapter 37   2015 THE SECRET WORLD OF CINDERELLA

Aged 66

'What's your excuse?'

'Yes, I certainly would like to play one of the Ugly Sisters in the pantomime,' I told the director when she phoned me a couple of days after the 'reading' in the local village hall. Our amateur dramatics society normally takes itself too seriously to do pantomime. Trollope, Shakespeare, Sheridan, yes – Cinderella, definitely not, and a surprisingly large number of members decided that they were 'resting' that autumn. I, on the other hand, could hardly wait: the boudoir scene, leading the community singing, old favourites - 'Sisters sisters, there were never such devoted sisters.' What larks! What japes!

The rehearsals began in September, one night a week in the village hall, and one night in the tiny schoolroom attached, because the bowls club had use of the main hall on Wednesday evenings. Weeks and months of rehearsals ensued, changes of cast, difficulties in finding singers and dancers, cast members missing from rehearsals and, irritatingly, habitually arriving late. I clearly remember the director in an over-loaded moment, rather futilely criticising somebody's actions on stage, when they were only reading in for an absent player.

The day of the costume fitting arrived, and we all dived into the dressing-up box. I wore a brassiere for the first time. Young female members of the cast kept playfully squeezing my 'falsies' until I threaten to reciprocate, and they immediately desisted and moved quickly away.

It seemed that it would be such fun when I first volunteered, but six weeks later at a rehearsal, the bubble burst. I lost my enthusiasm and asked myself why I was giving up all this time. Just learning the lines had taken me about fifty hours, and what with the dance steps, the high-pitched voice and the singing, I wished that I had never agreed to take on the part of Angina.

'We call her that because she's a real pain,' said the script, and I certainly did not like her. Fortunately I got on very well with Ewart, who was playing the other Ugly Sister, Verruca, who the script described as, 'Terribly easy to get hold of, but a bit of a nuisance, and terribly hard to get rid of.'

This was Ewart's fifteenth pantomime and he kept me on the 'straight and narrow,' suggesting jokes and ideas that were not in the script. He was very organised in the dressing room and brought his own garment rail, which he shared with me, and he had a props list for every scene.

Angina on the left and the much prettier Verruca on the right

The show never seemed to come together at the rehearsals in the village hall. Singers were rehearsing in one corner, dancers in another, the wardrobe mistresses were fussing around with pins in their mouths, and calling actors off the stage for fittings, while Ewart and I practiced a dance routine in the entrance hall.

Christmas arrived and we took a break for two weeks, then started again in early January. It was with some trepidation that I arrived for the technical rehearsal at the local arts centre theatre with its two hundred seats. Props would not work on cue. The fishing line needed to make a worm run across the stage would surely trip the dancers.

The dress rehearsal came: the dancers were late on stage for the boudoir scene, and then did not appear for the finale. Half the female actors were changing in the male changing room, but at least Ewart and I got some first-rate help with our bras, wigs, zips, ribbons, and, most important of all, our makeup, from the 'Fairy Godmother' appropriately enough.

Finally, the first night came, the theatre was only half full and four 'rowdies', possibly the worse for drink, barracked us constantly which threatened to put us off. Several members of the audience left and the cast were a little low after the show, although we outwardly retained our stiff upper lip - we are, after all, troopers. I was quite despondent when I got home, three months work, a half empty theatre and a group of people who had shown no appreciation. Why put in all that effort?

The second night, however, was a full house. Seventy children from the local primary school came with several of their teachers, and the atmosphere lifted to the stratosphere.

'It's behind you.'
'Oh, no, it isn't.'

'Oh, yes, it is.'

Verruca discovered the names of the two middle-aged male teachers and at the prescribed time said, 'Let's find some lovely, hunky men to be our partners.'

We, the sisters, moved into the audience and, after much close-up consideration and loud, and personal, criticisms of other cringing and petrified males, duly 'abducted' the two primary school teachers from their seats, led them to the stage, and danced with them in the ballroom scene. Their pupils were ecstatic, the teachers were secretly pleased, and it gave everybody something to talk about both in the class and the staffroom on the following Monday.

The third performance found Verruca and Angina in the boudoir scene, on stage in our bras, pants and dressing gowns, pretending to apply make-up while the chorus sings, 'Keep young and beautiful,' and eight girls performed a tap dance behind us. While looking darkly through my dressing table mirror, which had no glass in it, of course, I had a surreal moment as it framed the dimly lit and quizzical face of my wife, sitting in the front row with two of her friends, one of whom I had never been introduced to. Why did she let me do this? What sort of impression was I making?

The last night came and our lines disappeared like smoke, as we said them for the final time. As Verruca held up her invitation to the ball, Cinderella could see that, in large clear lettering on the side that was away from the audience, it said, 'Get your tits out Cinders, it's the last night.' Cinderella had a slight tendency to 'corpse' (laugh uncontrollably) in rehearsals, and we wanted to provoke it now.

In the second half, a woman barracked me once too often. I was battle-hardened now, and had been having 'If only I had said' thoughts about the heckling in the first performance. I moved to the front of the stage and called into the dazzle, 'It took me an hour in make up to look like this, love. What's your excuse?'

The theatre erupted into cheering and applause, the loudest that I had heard all evening.

There certainly is no business like it.

Two months later, my wife and I were walking past the local school and spotted the teacher who had been my dance partner. He was on playground duty standing quite close to the fence so, much to my wife's annoyance, I went over and introduced myself. He had never seen me without my hideous stage make-up and didn't recognise me at first. We laughed at our memories of the evening. A little blonde girl of about seven was standing nearby, engrossed in a puzzle that she was holding.

'Lucy, do you remember when I danced at the pantomime with the Ugly Sister? This is the man who I danced with.'

'Yes,' she said, pulling a wry face but not looking up. 'I thought you were going to kiss him.'

'I don't think so,' said the teacher rather taken aback, and – me feeling slightly awkward - we took our leave.

The End

AFTERWORD

I do not think that my life has been unusually interesting but, unlike most people, I have taken the time to write mine as a memoir. Over several years, before I retired, I made a list of many of the funny, strange or dramatic incidents that have happened to me during my life, put them into date order, and then decided which ones I wanted to admit to. Eventually, I wrote the stories and was lucky enough to have some of them published. Putting them all together and self-publishing them as a memoir has allowed me to feel that my experiences have been preserved and, although it might be of most interest to the immediate members of my family and possibly of some interest to my descendants, the magic of the internet allows me to offer it to anybody who wishes to read it.

If you feel that you could have done just as well as me, then you probably could - personally, I think that everybody should do it.

If you enjoyed this book please leave a review on Amazon.

My blog is at: rogerleywrites.blogspot.co.uk.

I would like to take this opportunity to thank all those who helped me to self-publish this book.

The copy and structural editing were performed by the multi-talented Nikki McDonagh, author, cat-fancier, teacher, photographer and guru to lesser mortals. She also formatted the work for Kindle and CreateSpace, and produced the photograph of the author. Her web site is: http://www.nicolamcdonagh.com.

The front cover image is taken from a chalk drawing by Angela Neill (if I have deciphered the name correctly.) She drew it about fifty years ago while we were teenagers, coming home from Aden on the SS Uganda. I am sorry to say that I have not heard from her since but I certainly wish her well.

The cover design is by the excellent Daphne du Muir.

Thanks to Edward Wilson for his encouragement and support and to my sons and step-sons who were kind enough to applaud my first attempts at travel writing, in the form of my emails from Beijing.

Finally, I would like to thank my wife Ann for her observations, good humour, wit and helpful suggestions.

March 2015

APPENDICES

Appendix 1 My letter of rejection for astronaut training from NASA about 1972

NATIONAL AERONAUTICS AND SPACE ADMINISTRATION
WASHINGTON, D.C. 20546

REPLY TO
ATTN OF: BPM

Mr. Roger Ley
69 White House Avenue
Boreham Wood
Herts, England

Dear Mr. Ley:

Reference is made to your inquiry regarding employment with the National Aeronautics and Space Administration.

Employment in the Federal Service of the United States is restricted by statue to U.S. Citizen, except in those cases where the non-citizen possesses unusually valuable technical or scientific knowledge or experience not readily obtainable from a citizen.

In view of this requirment, and after careful review of your qualification as described, it has been determined that we have no appropriate position suitable to your particular qualifications at this time.

Thank you for your interest in NASA's space effort.

Sincerely yours,

Owen P. Gallagher, Chief
Personnel, Administration Division
Office of Personnel

Appendix 2 Explosion on the Francis Holmes 1

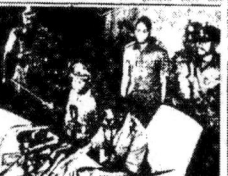

Appendix 3 Explosion on the Francis Holmes 2

Appendix 4 A family recipe which won the food competition in the Guardian

The Guardian | Saturday 17 January 2015

We'd love to hear your stories
We pay £25 for each Playlist, Snapshot, We Love to Eat or Letter to published. Email family@theguardian.com or write to **Family Life**, The Guardian, Kings Place, 90 York Way, London N1 9GU. Please include your address and phone number

We love to eat

Wet pizza, a favourite for five generations

Ingredients
1 onion, chopped
1 tomato, chopped
2 mushrooms, chopped
Mixed herbs and pepper to taste
150g cheese, sliced
2 rashers of bacon, chopped
150ml milk

Take an oven proof plate, spread the onion, mushroom and tomato on it and sprinkle on the mixed herbs and pepper. Place the cheese on top and then the bacon. The bacon should be last so that it will crisp. Pour on the milk. Transfer to the oven and cook at 220C for about 45 minutes.

The cheese will melt, spread over the onion and go brown. The bacon will crisp and the onion will simmer slowly in the milk, which will clarify in the process.

Take the plate from the oven and place it on top of another plate to save the table from damage. The meal is eaten with bread and butter which you cut up with a knife and fork so that you can soak up the delicious juices. It's also a meal that has many advantages: it is very tasty, can be prepared in advance and leaves almost no washing up.

Within my family we sometimes call it "Irish Pizza" because we suspect that it came over from Ireland with one of my maternal great-grandparents. It has been passed down five generation to my knowledge. Because of its simplicity it is a good activity to share with kids in the kitchen. It consists mainly of slicing cheese, chopping onion, tomato, mushrooms and bacon, pouring on milk and then transferring it to an oven for 45 minutes.

You can put your own spin on it by adding any other ingredients that would be found topping a pizza - such as olives, peppers, chillies, etc. You can leave out the bacon to make it vegetarian and you can easily vary what you put on each plate depending on your guests' preferences, so it is a meal that allows "individualisation".

My younger son is visiting me today and two plates of "wet pizza" are sitting in the oven waiting for me to turn it on when he arrives. He is home from a cycle trip to China (yes, really) and has been away for a year and a half.
Roger Ley

Before: wet pizza ready for the oven

After: wet pizza 45 minutes later

Appendix 5 Your baby has gone down the plughole (A mother's lament.)

(Writer unknown - London Music Hall Song)

As taught to me by my father W. G. Ley while he washed and I dried the dishes after dinner

A mother was bathin' her baby one day
The poor little thing in a terrible way
The mother was poor and the baby was fin
T'was nawt but a skellington covered in skin

While mother turned round for the soap on the rack
She was only one second, but when she turned back
"Oh, where is my baby?" in anguish she cried
"Oh, where is my baby?", and the angels replied

Your baby has gorn dahn the plug'ole
Your baby has gorn dahn the plug
The poor little fing was so skinny and fin
He should'a been bathed in a jug

Your baby is perfik'ly happy
He won't need a bath any more
Your baby has gorn dahn the plug'ole
He's not lost, just gone before

He's gone before

Appendix 6 List of articles previously published.

Chapter 3 1959 The train home from Dolgellau.
Appeared in the June 2015 issue of Best of British magazine under the same title.

Chapter 4 1961 I once met Tony Hancock.
Appeared in the March 2015 issue of Best of British magazine under the title, 'Hancock's Vodka Mouthwash.

Chapter 8 1967 I once met Graham Hill.
Appeared in the September 2015 issue of The Oldie magazine.

Appendix 4 A family recipe
Appeared in The Guardian in January 2015

Roger Ley

A HORSE IN THE MORNING

A memoir

Roger Ley was born and educated in London, and spent some of his formative years in Saudi Arabia. Having completed his initial pilot training and gained an engineering degree, he somewhat optimistically applied to NASA for astronaut training but, unfortunately, was not selected. He worked in the oilfields of North Africa and in the North Sea for some years before starting a career in teaching.

Since retiring, his writing has appeared in publications including The Guardian, The Oldie, Best of British, Jeff Hawke's Cosmos and various technical journals.

He was briefly a member of Mensa, but found the 'local chapter' a bit too weird.

He is married, has two sons and lives in Suffolk.

Roger Ley

A Horse in the Morning

Made in the USA
Charleston, SC
08 October 2015